BEYOND SURVIVAL

by

Drid Williams

PUBLISHING
1999

First Edition, first printing by **HIGH GROUND PUBLISHING**, a division of Northwoods Consulting, 6107 SW Murray Blvd., Suite 351, Beaverton, Oregon 97008.

Copyright © 1998 by Drid Williams.
All rights reserved. This book may not be reproduced in whole or in part, in any form, (except by reviewers for the public press) without permission from the publisher.

LCCN: 98-88419

ISBN: 0-9654915-8-7

Library of Congress Cataloging-in-Publication Data available upon request.
Printed and manufactured in United States of America.

Cover Photograph [photographer unknown] Drid Williams in "Forms I" (p. 117).

To my sister, Doris, whose unfailing love sustains and inspires, and to the memory of my father.

*If I am not for myself, who is for me; and being
only for my own self, what am I?
If not now – when?*

[Hillel, 'The Elder' - ?70 B.C. – A.D. 10?]

Contents

Chapters

One	'So foul and fair a day …'	1
Two	'Who can control …'	11
Three	'Childhood is a kingdom …'	23
Four	'Time past and time future …'	33
Five	'Just when we're safest …'	43
Six	'Footfalls echo in the memory …'	53
Seven	'From wrong to wrong …'	63
Eight	'So may the outward shows …'	79
Nine	'The thing on the blind side …'	93
Ten	'Not equal to equivalent to …'	105
Eleven	'I tell you that your daily bread …'	115
Twelve	'It's not just what we inherit …'	131
Thirteen	'I have lost friends …'	143
Fourteen	'And that sweet City …'	155
Fifteen	'Very nice sort of place, Oxford …'	169
Sixteen	'Reason is not come …'	179
Seventeen	'I wanted to live deep …'	189
Epilogue	'Not that the story need not be long'	197
Index		199

PEOPLE, NAMES AND PLACES
The Immediate Family:

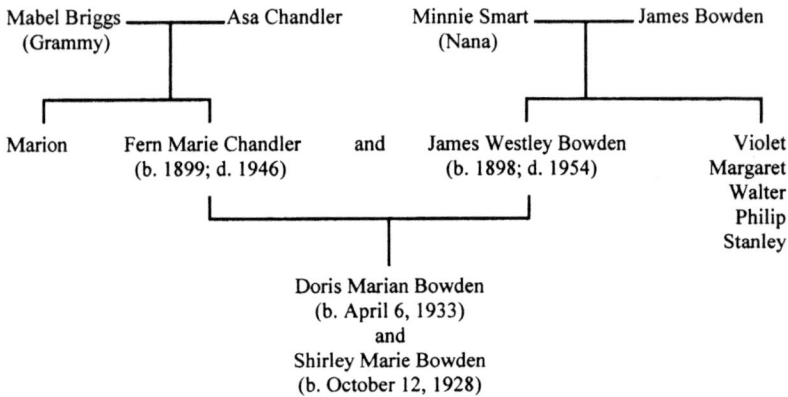

The Name Change:

Shirley married twice: the first time to Oliver P. Williams, whose last name she retained. She and Dorian (her second husband) danced under the name 'Drid and Dorian Ross'. Shirley changed her name to Drid when she was nineteen, having disliked her given name for as long as she could remember (see Chapter 3).

One day, idly thumbing through a magazine while waiting for a dental appointment, the name 'Drid' attracted her attention. It was the name of a heroine in a short story she doesn't remember. All she knew at the time was that she had found her real name.

A high school friend who later taught mediæval English at Stanford University told her the name was originally spelled 'Thryth', but the 'th' came into modern English as 'd' and the 'y' changed to 'i', hence 'Drid'.

An apocryphal story about Shakespeare's inspiration for *The Taming of the Shrew* has it that Thryth was a Welsh queen who was so mean and cantankerous that she was set afloat on the English Channel on a raft. The raft drifted to the coast of England, where she was picked up and taken to the reigning kinglet, Offa I, who married her. She turned out to be a decent sort after all.

EARLY PLACE NAMES AND LOCATIONS

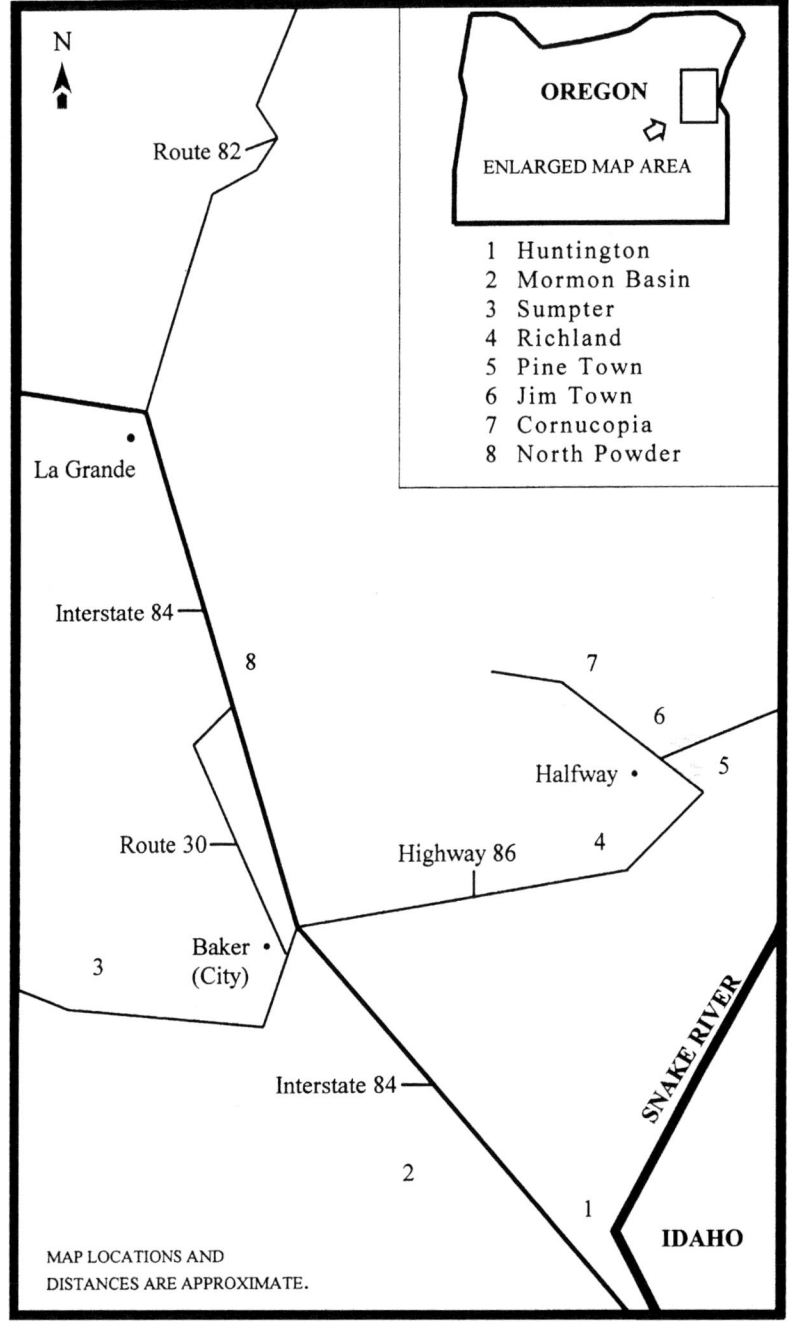

Foreword

It is a very difficult thing for a family when tragedy strikes. No outsider can fully understand the impact of such an event upon adults, much less the powerful effect it has upon children. Since each child is a different age, with different emotional and intellectual needs, they will each experience events in a totally different way. How they choose to deal with their individual pain and suffering will vary considerably.

There seems to be very little written about surviving trauma from a child's point of view. I recall thinking that, at thirteen years old, without a mother, I will turn out bad. My sister has written revealingly about how she coped with her personal tragedy. She has also shared as much as she could know about what I went through.

I think she has described the events that took place very well. I believe she has captured, and conveyed, the complete helplessness and futility we both felt at the time.

It is always easy to look back at the big picture of our parents' lives with the wisdom of hindsight, imagining what might have led them to the point they reached. Obviously, nothing can change the terrible reality that engulfed us all. But perhaps, by reading this story, the children of pain who read this book may learn, happily, that going far beyond survival IS possible.

Our Dad would have been pleased and proud of Drid's accomplishments. I know I am. Her story is very much a continuation of his story, as it is with all parents and their children. There is much of solid value and strength here.

Doris M. Irvine
Buffalo, Minnesota
September, 1998

Chapter 1

So foul and fair a day I have not seen.
[*Macbeth*, I, iii: 38]

With no introduction or preamble, the detective said, "Your mother's dead and your father killed her."

My voice was calm and controlled: "What did you say?"

"Your mother's dead and your father killed her."

"How do you know?" I asked, meaning how did he know what my father did or didn't do.

"You're Shirley Bowden, aren't you? You live at 2124 S.E. Yamhill Street?" he asked, with the stub of his pencil poised over a small notebook he'd taken from his inside jacket pocket.

"Yes. So what?"

"We've just come from there," he said, "Your mother is dead. She opened a trunk in the basement and a bomb blew her up. She's dead."

"Maybe so, but you said my dad killed her. He's not even in Portland. He left this morning for the coast to visit his brothers, Stan and Phil."

"We think he planted a bomb in the trunk knowing she'd open it."

"But you don't know that, do you? Where is my father?"

"He's on his way back to Portland" he said, "He's probably at the station downtown now. We got hold of the police, who called your father's brothers in Tillamook, Coos Bay or somewhere down there. You and your sister have to come to the station with us and make statements." He looked in the direction of the fireplace.

I sat there immobilized, trying to take in what I'd heard, aware of an intense anger invading my entire body — the kind of rage that stayed with me for ten years, only changing after four years of psychotherapy in New York City.

My body felt charged with wave after wave of energy: what would now be called an "adrenalin rush." I felt suspicious — wary — much as a cornered fox must feel when it hears baying hounds approach but has nowhere to go. It was the twenty-seventh of July, 1946. The circumstances around twelve midnight when this incident occurred were completely ordinary.

I was at Uncle Joe's and Aunt Violet's house, planning an outdoor picnic for friends from high school and the ballet school I attended. My younger sister Doris had been to an evening skating session at the Imperial Roller Skating Rink. She had already endured the experience of merciless questioning for three hours by the two strange men she turned up with at Uncle Joe's front door that night, but at the time, I knew nothing of her ordeal.

My uncle and I were sitting on the sofa in the big living room at his house when there was a knock at the door. We saw two men standing outside with Doris. I stayed on the sofa while Uncle Joe went to find out who the men were and what they wanted. He stepped outside onto the wide, shaded verandah. After a few minutes, he brought Doris and the two strangers inside, but his face was grey and contorted. He was in shock.

Although there were four other people in the room, I felt isolated. Uncle Joe and Sis moved to the fireplace out of earshot. The strangers took off their hats, one standing near the stairs by the front door on my left. The other loomed larger than life in front of me.

I still don't know who he was — only that he was an official from the Portland Police Department, but I will never forget his face or the clumsy, inept way in which he spoke. I stared at him. Several things happened inside: a split occurred in my consciousness. Even today, I have no idea how to describe it otherwise. It was as if I were sitting on the sofa looking at him, but at the same time I stood behind myself watching the whole scene. That split stayed with me during the next forty-eight hours. Even when it wasn't as clear as it was during the first moments of encounter, some kind of division of awareness persisted. One self participated in whatever was going on. Another looked on, as if watching a play.

The fact is that because of eight words spoken by a stranger, I was instantly catapulted into another level of consciousness that stayed with me throughout the ordeal of my father's trial for first degree murder in Portland, Oregon and his subsequent incarceration in the Oregon State Penitentiary as a 'lifer' in Salem. The memory of that July night has remained with me all my life.

The detective's words produced an emotional "flash-freeze" — a state of consciousness that both protected me and created deep misunderstandings between me and members of my family during the next few months, because my feelings were put "on hold." I've since learned that shocks of this magnitude cause many teen-agers to appear unfeeling and callous. They often become obstinate, sullen and reserved, as I did.

I looked toward my sister and uncle. Doris was crying. Neither had heard the conversation between me and the police official because they were too far away, but Uncle Joe saw me looking at him and walked towards the sofa, his arm around Doris protectively. The detective joined his partner at the bottom of the stairs.

I got up and went with Uncle Joe and Doris through the open sliding doors, through the dining room and into the kitchen at the back of the house. When we got there, Uncle Joe finally told Doris that Mom was dead. My young sister had been put through an awful experience. Not only was she bewildered and scared, she was the first person the police talked to. They treated her abominably.

They met her in front of the Yamhill house after calling her at the skating rink, ordering her immediate return. The friends she had been out with brought her home. She wasn't allowed to go into the house, nor was she told that her mother was dead. She didn't find that out until the three of us were in the kitchen. The police kept her, first in a police car outside our house for an hour, then for another two hours in a neighbor's house across Yamhill Street questioning her. She didn't understand what was going on. She was terrified by all the questions about mother and daddy. She cried because she was afraid. All she remembers of that night is fear.

"I'll go upstairs and phone Vi — tell her what's happened" Uncle Joe said. Auntie Violet was bedridden with tuberculosis contracted during her years of highschool teaching in Alaska, but she was able to travel to Halfway, Oregon, propped on pillows in the back seat of Uncle Joe's big sedan. She needed a change of scenery, and was with Auntie Margaret at the farm. "You get your things, Shirley, and I'll go to the police station with you and Doris. They want a statement from me too. You girls will stay here tonight and for the next few days 'til we find out what's going on." Uncle Joe looked at least ten years older than he had only a half hour ago.

I took my sister's cold hand, leading her from the kitchen to the coat closet under the stairs where I'd left my sweater and purse. She was trembling and the tears wouldn't stop.

"What's wrong?" she kept asking, "Where's Mommy? Where's Daddy? What's the matter? What're we going to do?"

"I don't know, Sis, but we have to get ourselves together now, so we can go and find out what's happened," I said, trying to comfort her as best I could until Uncle Joe came back. Actually, I was furious. Unlike my thirteen year old sister, I couldn't cry. I wouldn't give the two strangers the satisfaction, for a start.

Looking at the two men as I did when we passed by them to get my belongings from the closet must have indicated as much, because they shuffled their feet uncomfortably, looked at the ceiling and around the room and back at the both of us with a glance mixed with curiosity, pity and appraisal — a look I came to hate, but recognize all to well over the next four months.

I believe they tried not to stare at my sister and me, but I'm also sure they wanted to. I've always wondered what went through their minds then. They couldn't have liked what they had to do that night — or so I imagined.

Doris and I were two lower middle-class kids: I, nearly seventeen, shortly to attend Reed College on the outskirts of Portland. Doris was a brand new teenager, obviously completely broken up and in shock over the news of her mother's death. The detectives' jobs probably only rarely included such scandalous circumstances as a possible murder by bombing and this must have added zest to what I suspect were otherwise fairly dull lives.

I know the detectives were struck by the difference in Doris's and my reactions to the news they brought because my uncle later told me they'd commented about how sorry they felt for Doris and how puzzled they were that I didn't cry. "She must be a real tough cookie" one of them said to Uncle Joe.

I didn't cry that night, the next day or for several weeks after that, nor did I cry at my mother's funeral, but I woke myself up one night two months later at the end of September, sobbing as if my heart would break. That happened several times during the year following my father's sentence and it continued to happen for several years. Crying alone in the night relieved some of the immediate distress, for, as anyone knows who has experienced it, grief is physically painful.

Years later, I came to understand that the grief I felt was manifold: I think I understand what the German word, *weltschmertz*, means — a kind of "world" (*welt*) "pain" (*schmertz*). Closely connected with the grief I felt was a profound yearning. I longed for the time I had known before my parents began quarreling because I'd been able to ignore their feelings before the troubles began. Now, I couldn't ignore their feelings, nor could I escape from them. My parents were only half-real to me until they began to quarrel — until I had to recognize their darknesses.

In the Appendix to *Songs of Innocence and Experience. A Divine Image*, Blake says, "For Mercy has a human heart./ Pity a human face,/ And love, the human form divine,/ And Peace, the human dress." But he also says, "Cruelty has a human heart,/ And Jealousy a human face;/ Terror the human form divine,/ And secrecy the human dress."

I sobbed until my body was sore because I'd seen cruelty, not pity, look at my father through my mother's eyes. Jealousy, not love, transformed my father's face. Secrecy hid everything from view. It blinded my parents and everyone around them. I'd seen them tearing at one another but hadn't anticipated the catastrophic results. Torment and remorse, like two bloated rats, gnawed the bones of my crippled senses. Why couldn't I have *seen* what was coming; *done* something about it all? Most of all, why couldn't *they see* what they were doing? Why let a poisoned plant grow in our house?[1]

At the time, I didn't feel numb. Feeling numb is feeling something. I felt nothing inside and my body felt as it normally did. The only difference was that I became acutely aware of my surroundings and of what everyone said and did. I knew nothing that happened before those eight words were spoken would ever be the same, because I'd never see my life in the same way again. Nothing could be the same after the words were spoken, because no one — not family members, friends or acquaintances — ever saw me in the same way after I became a convicted criminal's daughter.

The three of us didn't know that night that the affair was already being referred to as "The Pandora Box Murder." The press had a field day. It was a melodramatic case and it was sensationalized to the fullest extent in newspapers and on the radio. My father was known (even in short items about his death eight years later) as "The Pandora Box Slayer." The incident was reported internationally, but the press didn't ultimately have it all its own way.

I gave the Hearst newspapers a black eye in court seven years later, winning a case of invasion of personal privacy against them. They were forced to change forever the format of the textbook example of yellow journalism they produced for newspapers all over the country, called *The American Weekly*. Needless to say, perhaps, experiences like these opened my eyes to the seamier side of social reality, exposing me to the nastier aspects of human character and behavior. On a personal level, I certainly found out who were my friends!

To me, nothing was the ever the same because of the drastic internal changes the detective's words initiated. Of course, there were external changes in family life brought about by Mom's death. For Doris and me, the changes were relatively simple:

---

[1] "I was angry with my friend/I told my wrath, my wrath did end./I was angry with my foe/I told it not, my wrath did grow." (William Blake, *A Poison Tree*).

there wasn't any real family life anymore. My mother ceased to exist and so did our family. After my dad's trial was over (he was sentenced to life imprisonment on Christmas Eve, 1946, narrowly missing the gas chamber, I was told, because of "us kids"), I stayed with Uncle Joe and Auntie Vi until I started Reed College that September, moving into a dormitory on campus.

For Doris, the changes brought several years of being passed around like an unwanted package no one could get rid of, from one foster parent situation to another, starting with Daddy's mother, Nan and her husband, Cy, in Bend, Oregon, where she stayed until the end of that year. Her years as a foster child ended with a premature marriage at age sixteen to a boy from Halfway, Oregon; Cliff Gentry. Their marriage made me extremely unhappy. Although it offered a solution of sorts to the family's problem of unwelcome responsibility, it wasn't a good solution. In any case, there was nothing I could do about it.

Nowadays, I'd call it "stress" resulting from my father's trial that prevented me from continuing at Reed College past the end of the first term. I quit in January, 1947, moving into a one room apartment with a kitchenette in northeast Portland.

I got a job at the Tik-Tok Drive-In, where I made good money in tips. The only family member who visited me during this time was Uncle Joe, and that was to a large extent surreptitious. Auntie Vi took a dislike to me because I "talked back" to her, because I smoked cigarettes and because she thought I should have stayed in college. She didn't like it because Eddie Crane (the step-son of Daddy's brother Phil's wife by a former marriage), had taken me out late on Christmas afternoon and we'd stayed overnight in a motel.

Nothing I could say would convince her — or Aunt Etta, Eddie's mother — that we hadn't had sexual relations, but we didn't. Eddie caught hell, of course, and he was sent away somewhere. I've never seen him since, but I will always remember his kindness and understanding and the fact that he held me all through that long Christmas night listening to my incoherent outpourings of sadness over my father's fate, and the fact that there was nothing I could do to help him.

Both aunts were angry with me because of what they imagined would happen to my relationship with Olly — Oliver P. Williams — the first man I married, whom I'd met at Reed College, who attended nearly every day of the two-plus weeks of my father's trial. They were wrong: nothing changed the relationship with Olly. We were married in June, 1947, but divorced a year and a bit later. His role as a sensitive, devoted and solicitous figure during the awful weeks of December, 1946, during my father's trial when we were both at Reed can't be overestimated. We'd met during rehearsals of a college production of a play, *The Silver Cord*. He worked as a stage hand and I had a small acting part.

Olly never humiliated me with pitying, curious or appraising looks. He was willing to have Doris live with him and me in Portland during the summer after we were married. He even organized an opportunity for her to live with his parents in California, even though the arrangement didn't work out. These were acts of a caring, concerned man, and to this day, I love him for it.

Olly's gentleness and honesty when I questioned him about what was happening in the court room were extraordinary. I couldn't attend the actual trial sessions because my sister and I were witnesses on my father's behalf. Although I had to be available through the whole thing, the only way I knew what was happening to my father was through Olly's accounts, later confirmed by what my father told me when I visited him in prison, and verified by what others said in endless familial rehashes of the trial.

It was because of Olly that I knew what my father said to the court just before he was sentenced: "I've always lived by the laws of this society, and if that society now feels that I owe them a debt, I've always paid my debts." I knew too that most, if not all, of the evidence the State's Attorney brought against my father was circumstantial.

My dad admitted constructing a bomb. He admitted placing it in one of his trunks in the basement of the house on Yamhill Street. He put it there, wrapped in a box, which was packed in another box, wrapped in brown paper, the whole approximately the size of a one and a half pound box of chocolates. The bomb was buried in the bottom upper right-hand corner of a footlocker, underneath clothing and other things. One of the reasons I later won the lawsuit against Hearst was because of these facts about the bomb. Newspaper accounts said that the footlocker/trunk my mother opened was itself wired to blow up, hence the Pandora's box theme, but that wasn't true.

My dad said he'd put the bomb in the footlocker intending to collect it a week or so later, after he'd arranged with one of his brothers to help him detonate it somewhere in the central Oregon lava deserts where no one would know about it, because he'd finally decided not to use the bomb on the person he really wanted to kill — not my mother, certainly — but the man whom I found out years later she was having an affair with; Frank Hokenyos.

I watched my father change so drastically over the year and a half before my mother's death occurred that he was hardly recognizable. When he came back from Adak, Alaska in early November, 1945 where he'd worked on a construction job making excellent money, he weighed about 180 lbs. — good weight for a man nearly six feet tall. He looked forward to enjoying the fruit of his labors with his wife and family. By the time he stood trial for my mother's death eighteen months later, he weighed about 160 lbs.

I saw the change start to happen in January 1946, when he started to be continually ill-at-ease and tense. From that time on, his body never seemed to relax. His face grew progressively darker by God-only-knew what twisted thought processes. He was a man transformed by jealousy and negative emotions into something I hardly knew, had I not watched the process as he and my mother made a battlefield out of their lives. My sister and I lived for many months in the no-man's land of our parents' mutual acrimony — their endless quarrels and accusations of each other.

By the time I was sixteen, since both parents used me as a "go-between" trying to justify their actions to one another and to me (as if I were both court of appeal and each one's personal *confidante*), I had come to some firm conclusions for myself. No matter what happened to me in future, I vowed, I would *never* let myself be overtaken by jealousy — my father's emotional *bete noir*, or indecision — my mother's downfall.

Daddy sent home every penny he made as a construction foreman in Adak. He made enough money to look after himself while he was away through playing poker and bridge. In fact, the circumstances that plunged my parents deeper and deeper into the abyss that resulted in Mom's death started with arguments over the money he'd sent home. My dad couldn't understand why only about half the money he'd earned was left. As usual, Mom either couldn't or wouldn't explain where the money had gone. I found out later she was in the early stages of menopause — a condition not as well understood in those days as it is now, which made a large contribution, I think, to our family's difficulties.

My father planned to use the money he thought he was saving as a down payment on a house. Unable to carry out his plan, he was determined to find out "what had gone on" as he put it. As he searched through the year he'd been away for answers, he thought he'd found at least one: a man my mother had a relationship with and upon whose dubious influence he eventually blamed everything.

During the weeks that preceded my father's trial, everything that led to my mother's death repeated itself in my mind as if it were a film playing over and over. What had Wes Bowden done that made him look like a murderer in other people's eyes?

Chapter 2

Who can control his fate?
[*Othello*, V, ii: 264]

Forever etched on my mind is what happened earlier that Saturday before Doris and I left the Yamhill house in the evening.

As usual, Mom went to work early in the morning. She left before eight, so she wasn't there when Daddy left for the coast to join his brothers. He packed his things, preparing for the trip, and around ten o'clock, he was ready to leave. He called to Doris and me, saying he wanted to go. Before leaving, he needed to talk to us and give us a good-bye kiss.

He knew his departure was for good. Divorce papers were served on him a few days before, even though he and Mom still shared the same bedroom. He was surprised, I think, that she had finally made a firm decision. For me, service of the divorce papers marked the welcome end of a long, tiresome process during which Mom dithered for several weeks, changing her mind. But, neither she nor my father stopped their interminable altercations; they needled and picked at one another ceaselessly.

She went to and from her lawyer's office, alternating between giving him instructions to initiate divorce proceedings, then withdrawing, so many times that I was thoroughly disgusted. I often accompanied her on these excursions, listening to her versions of the quarrels she was having that were prelude and postlude to the periodic visits.

In my eyes, Daddy didn't conduct himself with much more aplomb. That morning, for example, when he started what I feared was going to be yet another diatribe, I said, "Daddy, just don't start. It's all over. Right or wrong, there's nothing you can do. Just go to the coast and maybe we can all have some peace."

"You're right, Shirley. Maybe we all need some time to think, but there's one thing I want to say: don't touch any of my things in the basement — I mean the trunks, etc. — don't get into them, will you?"

"Why should we? That's a dumb thing to say. We've never bothered your things before. We don't do that in this family."

"O.K.," he said smiling, "let me give you girls a hug, and I'll be on my way."

We saw him to the door, then stood on the front porch until he reached the end of the block, turning out of sight.

"Thank heaven that's over!" I remarked to Doris as we re-entered the house, "now we can have some peace and quiet around here."

"But why did he tell us not to go into the basement?" Doris asked.

"He didn't say not to go into the basement, he just said to leave his stuff alone" I answered.

"What do you think he has down there?"

"I don't know and could care less. Probably nothing. You know how they've both been acting" I said.

"Let's just forget it, Sis. Go do something else. What he said makes no difference to anything. Anyhow, it's none of our business."

I went upstairs and buried myself in a book. I can't remember what Doris did, although she recalls meeting Mom downtown and returning home with her. To me, there was an all-pervading sense of relief and happiness knowing there would be no more quarrels and fighting.

Mom and Doris came home in mid-afternoon and both were in a good mood. We had an early supper which the three of us ate sitting around the small kitchen table. It was situated by a double window between two doors, one of which was behind me, leading into the dining room. Doris sat across from me with her back to the door opening onto the basement stairs. Mom sat between us at the end of the table near the kitchen stove.

Conversation was ordinary: Mom's pleasure over a gardenia and some small gift we'd given her, what we'd planned for the evening, etc., but the subject of Daddy's departure inevitably came up. Mom wanted to know when Wes had left the house that morning.

My sister said, "When he left, Daddy said we shouldn't go into the basement and …".

"That's not true!" I interrupted her angrily, almost shouting, not wanting to get Mom started talking about him.

"You're wrong" I continued, "all he said was not to bother his trunks and stuff down there. He told us not to get into anything, which was dumb because none of us *ever* gets into each other's stuff. Let's talk about something else."

"I wonder what he meant" Mom mused, as if to herself, as Doris got up from her chair saying, "Let's go see." She opened the basement door and started down the stairs.

I was around the table like a shot catching up with her on the stairs before she got a third of the way down. I stood one or two steps below her, blocking her way.

"You go on back upstairs, Doris, or you'll be sorry. What's the matter with you?" By that time, my mother had appeared in the doorway above.

This time I shouted, "Damn it, Mom! Make her come back upstairs. This is so stupid! He was just making up stories, as usual. Doris, if you don't go back upstairs, I'll do something awful," I said menacingly, advancing up the stairs forcing her back toward Mom and the open door.

"Oh, for pity's sake, let's forget it" Mom said, taking Doris's arm. She guided her back to the table.

"He's gone and that's what we've all been waiting for. Let's finish eating."

I sighed with relief as I returned to my place at the table. I would have done anything: created a scene, smacked my sister, risked my mother's rage and a possible whipping — anything — to prevent further discussion of my father. For once,

Mom appeared to be as anxious to avoid the subject as I was, and we finished our supper talking about other things.

It was that incident, of course, that the prosecution later made much of, building their case for motivation and intent upon what Daddy had said — or rather, on what Doris told them later that night he'd said.

In fact, no one knows (or will ever know) what went on in my mother's mind or why she went into the basement and went through Daddy's things that night. Several decades later, Doris and I speculated about her desire to find some bank statements my dad said "proved" something or another, but we will never know for sure.

It's difficult to convey how obsessed those two people were: each trying to prove disparate versions of their relationship. It's even more difficult assessing the damage done to Doris because of it. She suffered from an abiding sense of guilt for my mother's death for years because of what she told the police that night, which included seeing Daddy for an instant from a distance in the basement working at something with his gloves on.

What he was working at, she didn't know, nor did the police and the prosecuting attorney. But, as both Doris and I found out to our cost, such details are largely unimportant in the general scheme of things. I was convinced then and remain convinced now that my mother would have gone through Daddy's things regardless of anything either of us said or did, but all of this meant nothing to the detectives who kept at us at the police station into the wee hours of the morning.

"Your father wanted the three of you to open that trunk, didn't he?"

"Your father intended that Fern would find the bomb, didn't he?"

Their questions seemed endless. On the whole, they returned to the same themes over and over again.

All I could do was to keep saying, "No. We always respected each other's privacy. We didn't open each other's mail or get into each other's things. No. My dad wouldn't harm any of us. He was acting silly, but they both were."

"But your parents were fighting and arguing a lot, weren't they?"

"Yes they were, but that's normal. Don't all parents quarrel?" I'd ask.

"You don't know what my father thought or what my mother thought. Why keep asking *me* what they thought? They were both acting crazy; keeping notes about what the other said and did."

"Your father was angry because of the divorce papers, wasn't he?"

"Not so much angry as sad" I replied.

"But your sister says he told you not to go into the basement."

"Yes, that's what she *thought* he said, but he didn't. He never said "don't go into the basement." All he said was to leave his stuff in the basement alone and I told him that was stupid because we never got into each other's things."

"Then he knew what was going to happen, didn't he?"

"No, he didn't, and you stop saying that! I don't know what happened but I know my dad never wanted to hurt Mom or Doris and me. He loved us. That's why he finally left. He knew it wouldn't do any good to argue any more."

"But how can you say that when you saw him in the basement working on the bomb?" they asked.

"I never saw him in the basement working on anything and I never said that" I retorted hotly. "Why do you keep saying I did?"

Their questioning was relentless. They wanted to know what my parents had argued about, but I was suspicious because I could see that every question they asked pointed in one direction — establishing my father's presumed guilt. I didn't trust them. They couldn't keep my sister's and my stories straight, but they weren't the only ones.

In January 1947, a nine-page article about my parents appeared in a cheap pulp magazine called *Baffling Detective*. The article was written by Roderick Palmer, who called his story

'Booby Trap', sub-titled, 'Curiosity Kills'. Ironically, the article was included in a section called 'Fact Cases'. It was found in Uncle Marion's private files after he died in October 1976. Doris gave it to me in 1995.

This was only one of many sensationalized accounts of our mother's death that appeared in newspapers and magazines from August 1946 through February 1947. I regret not knowing about this story until fifty years later, because, in my opinion, the whole report is a fabrication that, interestingly, doesn't mention me or my sister. In 'Booby Trap' Mr. Palmer wrote:

> But perhaps more significant was the information supplied by a woman friend of the Bowdens to the effect that the wife had decided to get a divorce because of his insane jealousy and quarrelsomeness.
>
> "Fern told me that he accused her of having affairs with other men," the friend stated. "She said that she never had been interested in anyone else but that he wouldn't believe her. She was afraid that he might get violent during one of his fits of temper and that's why she planned to leave him."
>
> When Ferguson [Captain, Portland Police Force] heard this information he nodded with satisfaction. "That's the last piece of this jigsaw puzzle," he declared. "It fits in with the others and I think I know how the thing was done."
>
> Summoning the prisoner [my father], the Captain asked whether he was ready to tell the truth. When Bowden insisted that he had told all he knew the detective said:
>
> "All right, then I'll tell you what happened. You imagined that your wife was unfaithful and you hounded her to the point that she was going to get a divorce. When you couldn't talk her out of it you decided to kill her."
>
> "So you rigged up a booby trap and put it in the foot locker and then *told her not to open the locker.* You knew that her curiosity would get the better of her and that sometime when you were away from home she'd open it anyway."
>
> Ferguson paused to see whether his shot in the dark was having any effect. Aside from a faint smile on his lips the suspect remained impassive. ... He [my father] said that he had made the machine on the previous Thursday and Friday while his wife

was at work, and, *with almost a note of pride*, described the contrivance in detail. Bowden asserted that he had intended to deliver the booby trap to Trowbridge [Frank Hockenyos]. *He admitted that he had warned his wife not to open the foot locker*, but he denied doing this with the intention of getting her to open it out of curiosity. ...." (Pp. 73-4, italics added).

The last paragraph of Palmer's creation reads "The names Leslie Trowbridge and Burton Maierling as used in this story are not actual but fictitious to protect the identities of persons innocently involved in a murder investigation." There are other disclaimers that could have appeared, but facts aren't the real aim of authors who write this kind of trash.

The article is decorated, not only with photographs of my parents, but the Yamhill Street house, the footlocker and the basement. All it lacked was a photograph of my mother's mutilated dead body, but the author and editors decided to leave that to their readers' imaginations. Prominent, too, were captions for numerous photos of the police investigators involved. Under a photo of a man squatting in the dining room among broken dishes, one can read:

Explosion's Wake

A blast that rocked the foundations of the Bowden home, right, left in its wake this tangle of twisted furniture and broken glass being examined above by Captain Eugene Ferguson.

The "twisted furniture" shown in the photo consists of an overturned chair and a dining room table with its legs broken off. Another caption says:

Trap Artist

The outstanding police work of detective Leonard Shaffer, right, was partially responsible for this confessed slayer's admission that he had designed the infernal machine of death.

"The outstanding police work" was carried on (possibly by Shaffer and others) between one o'clock and five o'clock the morning of July 28th in the interrogation rooms of Portland's main police station. It consisted of questioning my sister, myself and my uncle. Other family members may have been involved that morning but if so, I was unaware of it.

What happened to my father while he was in police custody, I never knew. Nor did I know anything about the alleged "friend" who gave information about my mother's comments and attitude toward the divorce. The words that Palmer and many newspaper reporters used that I most objected to were "confessed slayer."

My dad wasn't a "confessed slayer" — he *was* a confessed bomb-builder. The police don't deserve credit for his admission he built the bomb as Palmer said they did. He never denied building it, nor did he deny harboring thoughts of killing the man he believed was ruining his home and his life.

Contrary to Palmer's version of the story, my dad did not admit he had "warned his wife" not to go into the basement (a) because she wasn't there when he left the house, and (b) according to him, he never said anything to my mother about the basement or his belongings. He told my sister and me not to meddle with his things, but that was all.

Something I thought about a lot as the weeks passed between the interrogation and trial was the fact that I didn't know how to talk about what I knew and what I thought was important. When I sat at the piano at my mother's funeral a week later playing Chopin études that I knew she hadn't really liked (in particular the 'Raindrop Prelude', which she found "monotonous and depressing") I knew her side of the family believed I was doing something especially appropriate to the occasion.

We were in Baker where Mom was buried (see map, p. vii) for over a week during her funeral, mainly because of Grammy. The worst part of being witness to my grandmother's grief was that she couldn't understand why her daughter's coffin couldn't be opened. She kept saying, "But I want to see Fern. I want to hold her one last time." She was in some state of what we would call nowadays, "denial." Opening the coffin was impossible owing to the condition of the body. I felt so sorry for her, but there was nothing I could do.

I felt I couldn't be honest with her because I'd been warned not to talk to her about how Mom died. She apparently understood nothing about the effects of bombs on human bodies. It's hard to see people you love hurting, and not be able to comfort them. By far the worst thing about the time we spent in Baker was the fact that, so far as Grammy and her family were concerned, everything was Daddy's fault.

Not one of them ever questioned that, which added to my problems because of the difference between the little I actually felt about everything and everybody and what I was supposed to feel. I felt guilty because I didn't feel any of the feelings people thought I should feel. That's the only way I know how to put it.

I was *supposed* to love my mother, and of the two parents, it was taken for granted that I loved Mom more than Daddy. My sister really did love Mother more. She hardly knew Daddy because he'd been away working so much of the time she was in grade school. All that Doris could think about at the time was her fear of what would happen. As far as she knew, children couldn't live without a mother. Years later, she told me she thought she would die too and I feel sure that in some sense, part of her did.

I vowed then that I would someday learn how to talk really well. I wanted to be able to express myself so I could avoid situations that made me feel unhappy, powerless and thwarted. I would get rid of the revolting feelings of impotence I had which, at the time, I thought were my fault.

My mother was dead and I hadn't really liked her. I didn't feel anything and the family said that was "un-natural." Like most kids my age, I'd secretly phantasized about Mom dying or going away somewhere. When she did die, I felt guilty; somehow, it was all my fault.

By the time I found myself playing the piano at her funeral, I understood in a vague, undefined way how inarticulate adults on both sides of the family were. Without realizing it, they repeated the same things over and over, or, when they talked to Daddy's defense attorneys and to each other, they would get things wrong and say things about my parents that, to me, were "made up."

The intense frustration and hostility I felt over this is impossible to describe. A lot of what family members (and others) said was nothing but speculation, or worse — they were really talking about themselves and their own feelings, not my parents. I learned how few people really think about what they say, even when a life is at stake.

I was immensely distressed because everything was thrown out of balance. Being somewhat of a musician and interested in drama, I thought many times of Shakespeare's Richard II:

> How sour sweet music is
>
> When time is broke, and no proportion kept!
>
> So is it in the music of men's lives" [Act V, v: 42].

Inside, I mourned my mother's death but, everything leading up to it was even more pathetic and saddening. I still regret the hatred leveled at my father by Mom's mother, who blamed everything on him; although working with Dr. Wadro in New York ten years later enabled me to understand *why* she thought the way she did, which helped.

Before Daddy's trial, she wrote an exceptionally damaging letter to the District Attorney in Portland, expressing the wish that her son-in-law pay for what he did with his life. Good Christian though Grammy was, when push came to shove, it was the Old Testament response of "an eye for an eye" that prevailed. As far as I know, her feelings about him didn't alter throughout the rest of her life.

The fact that I didn't cry at Mom's funeral was attributed by others who were there to the reality of my having to perform — a convenient myth. I couldn't cry because I was in a state of profound emotional shock. The double consciousness that began on that fateful Saturday night, however, saved me: a level of awareness that persisted through it all. The reason it saved me is that the observer-self somehow knew that the observed-self was enacting scenes that weren't of its own making. In any case, all the scenarios would eventually pass, even though everything seemed unreal — like *Alice Through the Looking Glass*. There was a huge gap between outer events and inner perception.

As I slowly closed that gap later on through the work I did in New York with Dr. Wadro, I came to recognize the horrific faces of the anger I carried with me for so long. The sense of loss I suffered was deep, but the rage I felt because of what my parents between them did to me and my sister was monumental.

Dancing helped me through a lot of this because I didn't conceal the anger I felt: I choreographed dances about it! However, it was only with therapeutic help that I slowly learned to hold my parents accountable for what they had done, no matter how unintentional or mechanical the acts and episodes that defined the ends of both their lives may have been.

Overall (and of equal importance to me), was the sense of injustice I felt over the treatment my father received in the press and at the hands of his lawyers, coupled with the injustice of his daughters being included in everything that had happened.

The only things to which my father ever confessed was building a bomb and having the intent to kill Frank Hokenyos. His words of caution and concern to Doris and me before he left for the coast to join his brothers that day were grossly misinterpreted, but they determined the shape of the next seven years of his life. To a large extent his words determined the shapes of Doris's and my life too. For the three of us, Richard the Second's words were true: time was well and truly "broke."

Mom was dead, and although I loved and respected her for taking care of me — for doing the best she could for Doris and me, I never really liked her. I don't think she liked me either. According to her standards, except for when I was little, I was not a likeable person and I didn't do acceptable things. I danced. I was an artist's model at the Portland Art Museum School, and I smoked cigarettes, for a start — and there were other things. She didn't like the way I dressed, nor did she like the way I combed my hair, especially for dance classes. How could I "streak my hair back so tight and tie it in a bun when I had such beautiful natural waves?" She told me several times that "they must have got the babies mixed up at the hospital" because she surely couldn't have produced someone like me!

Without exception, the memories I cherish of my mother are those from my earliest years, so it is to those I will now turn.

Chapter 3

Childhood is the kingdom where nobody dies.
[Edna St. Vincent Millay]

I loved the bright red 'Little Jim' wagon I got for Christmas, 1933. It was made of real metal, had real rubber on its wheels and a good strong handle. I pulled it everywhere filled with cherished toys. My favorites were the old brown leather-covered dictionary with its colored pictures of flags, trees and animals and my slate, box of chalk and eraser. The writing materials were more important to me than the raggedy teddy bear — although it was preferred over my dolls, one of which reposed untouched in a cradle upstairs in my bedroom. Another doll, arrayed in silken splendor, either sat in the child-sized rocking chair that had belonged to Grammy when she was a little girl, or was propped unceremoniously on the chest of drawers.

Last but not least, there was the Shirley Temple doll. I had ambivalent feelings about that doll because, including me, there were nine little girls named Shirley in the second grade. My mother wasn't the only one who named her daughter Shirley, but the others didn't have naturally curly hair, nor did they fit the image of the child star as well as I did. Every morning, I brought the hairbrush to my mother and my hair was curled around her finger so that I looked the way she wanted me to. I even had a pink georgette dress, copied from one of Shirley Temple's dresses. I liked the dress, but hated the name, Shirley. I never called myself that.

"Mama, why isn't my name Elizabeth, like the princess?"

"Because I didn't want people to call you 'Beth' or 'Bess'. I almost named you Charlotte, but then people would have called you Lottie and I don't like that."

Shirley was my name and Shirley it remained until I was nineteen and found my own name, Drid.

The red wagon not only carried favorite toys, it held an assortment of old muffin tins, miniature pie-pans, a few empty jam jars and some old knives, forks and spoons. Even though we had hot and cold running water in our house and 'proper' bathrooms, there was a water pump in the spacious backyard near the garden shed and garage, and what a wonderful place that was!

Endless childhood games took place there in the company of neighborhood kids: the Teboe children, who lived "kitty-corner" across the street at the end of the block; David Lanning, whose mother often visited, and sometimes left David to play with me under my mother's watchful eye. Donna Miles was a frequent playmate because her parents were in the American Legion, along with my parents and the Lannings.

I recall that we children made endless mud pies. We played hide and seek in the house and outside, and, for a few months, we played with the little gray jackrabbit my dad brought home one day. It was wild and had gotten caught somehow in a load of lumber. It grew quite fast and was a household favorite until Christmas, 1934, when it mysteriously disappeared after chewing a hole in Daddy's new sport coat jacket and ruining a pair of Mom's silk stockings.

When it stormed, I and my friends hid under the washing machine on the back porch: a place I was convinced kept us safe from thunder and lightening.

My mother, Lillian Lanning and Elaine Miles, along with other Legion Auxiliary friends, often traded off looking after us. I sometimes stayed at David's or Donna's house while my mother was away for the day. When all the mothers played cards or something, an older girl, Mary Pieffer, would look after me. Mary came when there was just me and baby Doris, who wasn't any trouble because she slept most of the time.

I loved the times when Mary came, because she could make paper dolls. She had a real talent for drawing, not only the dolls, but the pretty clothes they wore. We'd play paper dolls for hours. Mary made larger dolls for me because they were easier for little fingers to handle without tearing. Mary had 'Lillian', a special doll with a whole big envelope stuffed full of clothes. I could look at Lillian but couldn't touch her, as she was Mary's favorite.

We played many games with those dolls; they took trips, had dinner parties, went on dates, swimming parties and camping. They dressed up to go to church, had picnics in the park, went to movies and dances. Everything Mary or I could imagine, those paper dolls did! A few years later, when I was an avid reader of the Oz books, I often thought about Mary Pieffer, through Dorothy's adventure with Miss Cuttenclip,[1] who lived in a whole village made out of paper in Oz.

My childish world was filled with other children and with interesting adults, one of whom was 'Old Leon', an ancient Chinese with a white hair, a wispy beard and twinkling eyes, who always brought lychee nuts, candied ginger and thin, sugary strips of dried coconut. He brought pretty embroidered silk kerchiefs for Mama, and, one time, he brought a pair of embroidered red silk slippers for me. Mama said he was a friend of her family when they lived in Galena, Oregon when she was a girl.

Our house was often visited by members of my father's 'clan', as it was called. Grammy, Granddad, Uncle Marion and Auntie Georgia visited at least once a week, and my parents had parties for their many friends, especially those who regularly played bridge with them.

Bridge parties were occasions where my mother shone, not only as a good bridge player, but as an excellent cook and hostess. She was proud of the party buffets and dinner tables she graced — and rightly so. I remember a bridge game specialty of hers — a confection (made from scratch, as nearly all bakery goods were in those days) called 'Walnut Cream Pie', for which I cracked and shelled the walnuts, digging out the rich nutmeats with a silver-plated nutpick.

The walnut pie had to be carefully made in a double boiler on the coal-burning stove, and so did the chocolate pie with the graham cracker crust, for which I was allowed to use the rolling pin, happily reducing the crackers to fine crumbs.

---

[1] In Frank L. Baum's *The Emerald City of Oz* (1910, p. 117). In my edition, the story is Ch. 10, 'How the Cuttenclips Lived' pp. 100-113.

Her Waldorf salad was famous (it needed walnuts too), and her potato salad always disappeared first at American Legion dinners and picnics over which she often presided. Her salads were favorites at family picnics and annual berry-picking trips into the wooded hills that surrounded Baker valley (see map, vii).

I helped my mother and Grammy cook and 'can' (which is what they called it). For they and all my aunts — in fact, all the women I knew — preserved fruits and vegetables, made pickles and relishes, jams and jellies, and applesauce. Our basement at the Washington Street house smelled earthy and a bit musty, but it was a wonder to behold — at least to my child's eyes — for the light was dim, but not so dim it didn't illuminate the rows and rows of golden Hood River peaches and ivory colored pears, spicy applesauce, crunchy green dill pickles, bread and butter pickle slices, tiny green peas, yellow sweet corn, ruby tomatoes and berries. We picked the purple-black wild huckleberries ourselves, and the huge heart-shaped strawberries, plump raspberries, blackberries and pale green gooseberries which Grammy grew in her garden, all of which usually ended up in splendid pies. Many times, we traveled to outlying farms around Richland and Baker, where we could pick all we wanted for pennies a basket.

When I was seven and eight, living with Grammy and Granddad, I made pocket money by picking gooseberries which I sold to neighbors for twenty-five cents a pail. Maybe that doesn't sound like much now, but in those days, five cents bought a double-scoop ice cream cone from the Shreeks Ice Cream wagon; a penny bought a whole handful of candy — not as good as my mom's nut-filled fudge and divinity, of course, but bearable when that, or the shiny, cream-colored taffy we made and pulled, wasn't available. A dime bought entry to the Saturday matinee at the Baker movie theater: a wonderous place all white and gilt with deep red carpeting and snuggly plush seats.

The peaches, pears and delicious apples we bought for twenty-five cents a bushel. Traveling to the orchards to buy them (which often meant camping or staying with friends in outlying towns overnight) always meant exciting excursions. I'll never forget seeing boxes of Hood River Delicious apples on display in shop windows in New York City the first time I went there. The huge red and yellow fruits were individually wrapped in paper and arranged in attractive designs in their shallow wooden boxes. My mouth watered, but they cost from ninety-five cents to a dollar-and-a-quarter apiece! Remembering childhood bounty, I could scarcely believe the prices! I'll never forget my disappointment either, when, homesick, I ordered a piece of mincemeat pie in a New York restaurant. There was no meat in it. Eastern mincemeat pie was just candied fruit and citron. I only took one bite.

Mama's eleven-inch mincemeat pies were not only gastronomic delights, they were an annual autumn production during my childhood which included Daddy and the men in his and my mother's family. You see, the meat in real mincement was venison (the neck meat of deer, mixed with apples, cloves and raisins) which my dad hunted and killed every year during deer season.

All the women I knew were excellent cooks and bakers. All the men I knew until I was eleven or twelve years old were hunters. We ate venison, elk, rabbit, wild duck, partridge, quail and pheasant. These were special, of course, supplementing the beef, pork, and lamb — our more usual fare.

I will always remember mother, presiding over a perfectly set 'company' dinner table, beautifully groomed and dressed, clothed in a black velvet evening gown (her favorite), with her silvery white hair gleaming in the candlelight. For some reason unknown to me, her hair had turned completely white when she was twenty-five. Father was unforgettable, too, immaculately turned out in a tux or dark business suit, carving a roast of beef, a turkey, pork spareribs or ham.

Mother was a delightful hostess. Father matched her skills as an excellent host who sharpened the carving knives he used at the table to cut perfect slices of meat. He was amusing too, for as he performed the ritual of honing already razor-sharp knives, he made our dinner guests laugh at his well-told jokes, anecdotes and stories.

He and my mother were rightly proud of these occasions and of the table to which they had both contributed. The spotless white linen tablecloth and napkins were suitable backgrounds for the gold-rimmed china, gleaming monogrammed silverware and stemmed amber water goblets, wine glasses and candlesticks.

The amber glass and white linen combination was further enhanced at the end of the meal when the dinner dishes were removed, either by Mary Pieffer or a neighborhood woman who had come to help out. Mama poured coffee in the set of black coffee cups that matched the black dessert plates holding wedges of one of her fabulous pies, featherlight cakes or some other equally delicious treat she'd concocted. The dessert dishes were accompanied by lead crystal candy and nut dishes cunningly shaped into small baskets.

The meat my dad brought home from hunting was all kept in one of the storage lockers the local ice company rented. In those days, we had an 'ice-box' (not something everyone had) in the kitchen, but it wasn't big enough to store half a steer and half a pig that my dad helped my uncles butcher when we visited his sister, Margaret. Her's and Uncle Raleigh's farm (the family called it a 'ranch') was in Halfway, Oregon.

I can't recall my parents buying meat in a butcher shop for the first seven or eight years of my life. Meat was something we brought home from "the locker." Sometimes, if daddy had pre-packaged some of the hanging carcasses, the Shreeks man brought a package or two from our locker when he brought the block of ice for the ice-box once a week — more often in summers — while we were at the Washington Street house.

I learned so many things from our summertime visits to Uncle Raleigh's and Aunt Margaret's place. Milkmen brought milk to our house in Baker everyday in quart bottles — white on the bottom and pale yellow at the top, because the light cream rose. The heavy whipping cream for Mom's pies and desserts came in pint bottles, but I knew where milk really came from because I'd been to Halfway (so-called because it was halfway between Pine Town and Jim Town), and the first major stop past Richland, on the way to Cornucopia, where I went to school in fifth and sixth grades (see map, p. vii).

I helped herd the cows into the barn when we stayed at the ranch, and I knew what 'milking' was, although I never learned to milk a cow because I was both fascinated and scared by the big animals. I helped put the milk into the separator, turning the handle — two of my older cousins and I took turns — then I saw the milk go into big sterilized metal cans to be taken to the Co-op, where Uncle Raleigh sold it. He also sold the heavy cream that wasn't used for family consumption.

Grammy and Granddad always had two or three cows but that seemed different from my uncle's herd in Halfway because Granddad's cows had names and were more like pets. Uncle Raleigh's herd of twenty-five or thirty animals were nameless and lacked personalities. Nevertheless, it was from Grammy and Auntie Margaret that I learned about making cottage cheese. I took my turn at churning butter and turning the handle of the squeaky ice-cream machine revolving in its bucket full of rock salt. Both farms had hen houses, thus gathering eggs taught some important lessons. And it was fun — all of it — because the barns and hen houses smelled so good, and the hens sometimes laid their eggs in the oddest places!

I'll never forget learning where eggs came from as I watched a white leghorn hen lay an egg when I was six or seven. The hen probably picked the place behind one of the cow's mangers in the big barn so she'd have privacy, but the silly bird didn't know her backside was fully exposed to my interested view!

In Halfway, with Aunt Margaret's children, Darlene, Helen and Beryl, Doris and I climbed in the barns and tumbled in the sweet-smelling hay. We climbed green, fruit-scented trees in the apple orchard and took cold lemonade, iced tea or hot coffee to the men working in the fields. This was exciting, because we often got to ride an old workhorse, Toby, out to the fields instead of having to walk. Only one cousin could never play with us: Jackie, who was older than Darlene, but had never walked. She was afflicted with spastic paralysis when she was a toddler and had to stay in the house all the time.

We children pulled carrots, potatoes, onions and lettuce. We picked beans and peas, and gathered squash and melons for the enormous meals my aunts cooked for the family when the

Bowden clan gathered. We helped with meals for haying and threshing crews during the late summer harvests, too.

After we pulled the vegetables, we'd wash them using the garden hose and after we picked string beans, we'd 'snap' and wash them, or we'd shell peas. It was a child's chore to keep wood and kindling in the wood-boxes, because there was no central heating, either in Baker or in Halfway. We fetched things from the 'cooler' which was an underground cellar, or the 'ice-house' where milk, cream, cheese, and other perishables were kept along with hams and bacon.

We helped wash and iron clothes and had no idea what a laundromat was. I even helped Gram make soap a couple of times. My mother had a washing machine with a hand-turned wringer. There were no such luxuries on the farm, which meant we used washboards and wrung things out cooperatively. After everything was clean, we'd hang it all on the clothes lines in the backyard, which were strung near the outhouse. The farm didn't have indoor toilets, although it did have a pump in the kitchen for water.

I learned how to cook more or less by osmosis, because all the children had to help. We didn't really think of it as work — at least, I didn't — it was just part of the day's activities. We'd set the table — often for as many as twenty people for dinner, which was in the middle of the day. There were rarely less than eight or ten of us at every meal, because even when it was only the Koopman family (Auntie Margaret, Uncle Raleigh, Jackie, Darlene, Helen and Beryl) and my sister and I, there were eight. If someone dropped by, or if any of the farm hands ate with the family, there were more, but there was always room for extra people and plenty of food to go around.

Besides chores, there were lots of other things to do at the farm that were fun. How Aunt Margaret ever did it, I'll never know. She would sometimes organize entertainments after supper in which all the children participated, and she did too. These were especially elaborate when the Bowden family were all there, and we recited poems, sang songs, danced, and told jokes. Either Aunt Margaret or Aunt Hazel played the piano. My dad and a couple of uncles played the guitar; but best of all were the playlets that Auntie Margaret made up, for which we had costumes made of crépe paper. She made our costumes, sewing them on her old treadle machine.

We never lacked entertainment: we played double and triple solitaire, Old Maid and 'Fish'. We read aloud to each other; we popped corn and made extraordinary popcorn balls, which, thanks to Auntie's bottles of food-dye, were every imaginable color, including blue-green and purple. We made taffy, which had to be pulled, of course. That produced gratifying, although messy, sweet-buttered hands. We made fudge which had to be beaten until our small arms ached, then we endured waiting until it cooled — agonizing in anticipation. Our impatience invariably resulted in a pan full of candy with fingermarks 'round the edge where we'd poked it to test how hard it was.

Not many people had as happy an early childhood as I had, but people who knew Doris and I later found this hard to believe. When Mom died, I heard people say over and over to my aunts and uncles, "You must've known something like this was coming" — but nobody did.

Through the chaos following Mom's death and the weeks that plodded monotonously towards Christmas Eve, 1946 — the day that marked the end of Daddy's trial — I took frequent refuge in rememberance. It wasn't an escape because the double consciousness always kicked in. Remembering was just a practical exercise in psychological survival.

Chapter 4

> Time past and time future
> Allow but a little consciousness.
> To be conscious is not to be in time
> But only in time can the moment in the rose garden
> The moment in the arbour where the rain beat,
> The moment in the draughty church at smokefall
> Be remembered; involved with past and future.
> Only through time time is conquered.
>
> [T.S. Eliot, *Burnt Norton*, 5]

Remembering was a game I played with myself so that I wouldn't go crazy, especially when I had to be with the family. Everyone knows life has to continue, even when something terrible has happened. Family members did the best they could, but they hardly knew what to say to each other, much less to a seventeen-year old. Maybe the worst part of what occurred in our family was that communication almost stopped.

Because friends from the ballet school and the Art Museum were uncomfortable when I was around, they stayed away. Except for Olly, nobody at Reed College seemed aware of my situation. The only social life I had was there. From October, 1946, until the middle of December, I was coached periodically by Daddy's defense attorneys about what to say at the pending trial — a process which I found tedious and boring. My reaction was to retreat into an inner world.

Remembering was a way of making my life important. The game worked like this: when I saw anyone — my cousin Helen, for example, I recalled everything I knew about her. That way, she became more than she appeared to be in whatever present moment we shared.

I remembered her playing marbles in Halfway — she was always good at that, although she kept busy grooming one of her calves whenever she had extra time. She belonged to the 4-H which meant she raised, then exhibited prize yearling steers at the annual county fairs. 'The Fair' was always a busy time, and Helen was the star of the show because she had exhibits. The rest of us watched enviously while she prepared for the big event. Sometimes we tried to help, but she didn't appreciate that much because nobody could do anything well enough to please her.

We didn't clean the animal's hooves properly, nor did we know how to comb and curl its tail. We didn't polish its horns hard enough, nor did we apply the clear fingernail polish so that hoof and horn gleamed perfectly clean and bright. We couldn't wield a curry-comb as expertly as she did, and she never let me, at any rate, forget it! My citified accomplishments didn't impress Helen at all.

She scoffed at "kids from the city who don't know *anything*," but I got my own back when she came to Baker by teasing her about wearing overalls all the time and not knowing how to behave with my friends. She eventually came out on top of the teasing contests though because once (to teach me a lesson about everything I didn't know), she let me lead one of her prize steers in a parade.

The calf assigned to me for this event was a black Angus steer called Tuffy. To me, it was absolutely huge. Compared to my eighty-pound body, its several hundred pounds of black bulk and switching tail looked like the devil himself! Helen looked after Wimpy, winning the Reserve Grand Championship at the State Fair in Portland that year with him. Wimpy was a red and white Hereford that seemed somewhat less menacing than the creature I had charge of.

Uncle Raleigh handed me Tuffy's lead-rope, telling me to make him keep still. Above all, he mustn't wander off to the nearby grass across the street — as if I could have prevented him from doing that or anything else he wanted! Adding to my discomfort, Tuffy dropped a steaming, smelly pile of dung on the cement in the parking lot where we stood.

The worst moment, however, was when he stepped on my left foot. Fortunately, I wore a pair of sturdy Oxford shoes, but what could I do? I wanted him to get off my foot. I pounded hard on the ebony flank of that steer with my right fist — I couldn't let go of the rope in my left hand — but all I got for my trouble was a mild stare of astonishment from his huge brown eyes and a rough tongue sloppily licking my arm. Tuffy thought I was playing with him! As Helen was nowhere in sight, I yelled at Uncle Raleigh, who told me to shut-up. I finally got across to him that I couldn't get Tuffy off my foot.

He came to the rescue, blaming me, not the steer, for my misfortune. Had I been brought up properly on a farm, he said, I'd have known what to do, but by that time, the parade had started. Tuffy led me sedately down Main Street along with the rest of the livestock, quite enjoying the drums and the band music, I think. P.S.: my foot was black and blue for a week, but thanks to the Oxfords, nothing was broken.

That was the only time in my life I was in a parade, but thinking about Helen and Tuffy led to remember many Fourth of July and Memorial Day parades, because Daddy was a drum major for the American Legion Drum Corps.

His uniform was ever so grand! It was white with gold buttons and epaulettes and there was gold braid that swung as he marched. I was impressed because the braid never got tangled up with the three-foot-long silver baton he carried. He threw it up in the air and did wondrous things with it. He looked so elegant with the magnificent black fur shako on his head that added at least fourteen more inches to his height. He had a terrific sense of rhythm and loved all kinds of music. The Drum Corps participated in nearly all the local parades, and when I was three and four years old, I thought the parade on Columbus Day (October twelfth) was really in honor of my birthday!

There were always more things to do in Baker and Halfway than we had time for. To this day, I have difficulty understanding the obvious boredom of some of my friends' children, who don't know how to amuse and entertain themselves or each other. Members of the Bowden side of the family either sang or played music. Everyone had a piano, and, except for the wind-up Victrola we had at the Washington Street house, music was home-made. Daddy's small collection of records contained the only recorded music we knew, apart from the radio.

The first music I ever remember hearing was Bizet's *Carmen* (my Dad's favorite music was opera). I was early acquainted with Tännhauser and other Wagnerian operas, and with Enrico Caruso's voice. We also had some wax records of Fritz Kreisler and a couple of pianists whose names I don't remember. However, Liszt, Brahms, Schubert, Tschaikovsky, Bach and Beethoven were all familiar names to me as I grew up, as were those of Homer, Plato, Shakespeare, Wordsworth, Whitman, Tennyson, and Byron — and Conan Doyle, thanks to my dad, who loved good words as much as he loved good music. In fact, my father is the only man I've ever known who, after eight hours on the work-end of a jackhammer at Shasta Dam, could come home and read Plato's *Republic* or the *Iliad* and the *Odyssey* to his older daughter. We lived in Redding, California then, near Shasta Dam which was being completed in 1941 when the Pacific War started.

Daddy also taught me how to bait a hook, fish for trout and how to handle, clean and shoot a rifle — a Remington '22'. I remember him poring over the blueprints for a naval base (Camp Farragut) in Spirit Lake, Idaho, where we lived for awhile after we left Redding, California before moving to Portland. He was foreman there for a gang of steamfitters who had to follow blueprints — often wrong in terms of what was practical.

As much as he loved books, he had nothing but contempt for those whose only knowledge came from them. Although they never knew it, architects who hadn't mixed cement, used a lathe to thread steam pipes, or handled a wrench were the butt of sarcastic jokes and streams of colorful invective night after night as he wrestled with the problems of translating their drawings into material reality.

Seeing my sister again before Daddy's trial started gave me an opportunity to remember the happy childhood years we shared before we came to Portland where all the trouble began. We lived in places like Cornucopia, Oregon (now a bonafide ghost town), Sumpter, Oregon, where Daddy operated a rock and gravel crusher, and a place called 'Mormon Basin', which was a few miles from Huntington, Oregon. There my father had a gold mine that he worked, mainly during summers or whenever he could get away from the laborer's jobs of all kinds he took to support us.

He had an interest in a deed to some property left over from Great Grandpa Bowden's salad days — property adjoining a legendary eastern Oregon gold mine called 'The Rainbow' out of which fortunes had been made at the turn of the century. My dad believed (along with several others) that a vein of ore belonging to the Rainbow might run somewhere beneath the family's unused land. Anyhow, it was worth a try.

Anything was worth trying during the aftermath of the Depression. In one way of looking at it, we had nothing to lose, so, virtually single-handed, Dad sank a shaft on the Mormon Basin property. This meant that we lived for a few months of 1935-36 in a mill-board and tar-paper shack that somebody (possibly grandpa James Bowden or his father) had erected in the past.

Some of the best times I remember with Doris were in Mormon Basin because the two of us were on our own. Nobody lived nearby. Our house (such as it was), was situated in the middle of a sagebrush desert about half a mile from the mine shaft site. It was at least fifteen miles to Huntington, where we brought in food and other supplies over a narrow, tortuous dirt road that hemmed the eastern edge of a deep canyon.

We carried water several times daily to the house from a spring situated about one long city block away. The water was transported in galvanized buckets and I helped Mom with that. We'd also carry cold water from the spring to Daddy at the mine-site. He'd drink deeply from a long-handled dipper that Doris carried because she was too small to manage a water-bucket. He'd take a little break, smoke a cigarette and talk to us about our day. He'd ask how Fern was doing, what we had been doing etc. Then he'd give us a hug and go back to work.

Lots of things in our life at Mormon Basin revolved around buckets and tubs. There was always a bucket of cold drinking water sitting on the porch-step of the shack in the shade, its blue and white dipper hanging from a nail on one of the support posts of the porch roof. There was a big galvanized tub for washing clothes outside, which did double-duty for

Doris's and my Saturday night baths. On those occasions, it sat near the stove where the hot water was. Even now, I don't know how or when my parents bathed, although I know they did, because they were always clean and tidy — except for my dad when he came home from work at the mine. He had a special wash-basin with soap and towels arranged on a table outside and behind his and Mom's bedroom. Perhaps that's where they bathed as well: in their room after my sister and I were asleep.

I was equally mystified about sleeping arrangements when Uncle Joe, Nan and Cy, Uncle Stan or other family members came to help Daddy with the mine. I think they solved the problem with tents pitched behind the house, or near the spring. I seem to remember army cots, but wouldn't swear to it. Sometimes the men slept outside in sleeping bags under the old flat-bed truck. Doris and I went to bed early, as everyone got up with the sun. Eight o'clock was bedtime and we were ready for it.

All the hot water we used was stored in a side-tank attached to the wood-burning stove and in the huge tea-kettle whose low simmering murmur always provided a soothing background to household activites. The stove was located in the kitchen area on the left side of the one large room where we lived, ate, slept and played when we weren't outdoors. Mom and Daddy had a separate lean-to bedroom and storage space off the one main room at the back. We washed-up and did dishes in a large basin on a long kitchen counter on the left side of the room near the stove.

At night, we had candles, kerosene lamps and pressure lamps, one of which lighted the way to the outhouse where I'd get fascinated looking through the catalogues. I've always wondered if the administrators of Sears-Roebuck and Montgomery Ward's stores were aware of how much toilet paper they supplied to the many people who couldn't afford such luxuries during the Depression. The huge catalogues were widely known as "wish-books." When they were well-thumbed, or we got new ones, they served their humbler purpose.

Inside the house, Doris and I sat on benches on either side of the one large table which served as a dining table, card table, sewing table, writing desk — or anything else that was needed. The table was constructed like City Park picnic tables in Baker, but it seemed different because Daddy had a wooden 'captain's chair' with arms at the head of the table and Mom's straight chair was at the other end. To my sister and me, life at Mormon Basin was a kind of extended picnic, although I'm sure it wasn't that to either parent, especially Mom.

Perhaps Mother's later contempt for anything that wasn't useful or comfortable emerged from her experience of these times. If the mine had paid off, then I feel sure the deprivations she went through would have been considered worth it. Because it didn't, her experience merely added items to a long list of grievances generated by the Depression. She wore the same winter coat and hat for six or seven years; she had no new clothes and she lost all of her pretty furniture and comforts of the home she'd had when she was newly married. There's no doubt she was subjected to deep disappointments, but how they affected her later on when the hard times were over, I simply don't know.

I remember her sitting in her rocking chair near the kitchen stove while she darned socks, sewed hems in dresses, buttons on shirts, and such. Her chair and the stool beside it where she put her sewing basket were the only other pieces of furniture in the room, except for the bed where Doris and I slept.

Sis and I had a row of six wooden orange crates in which underclothes and other belongings were kept. Our parents had a large chest of drawers and a big bed in their room. What we would've done without those double-sided orange crates I can't imagine! All our treasures — the rocks we collected, hair ribbons, dolls and trinkets, a few books and things were stored in them. Dresses, sweaters and coats hung neatly on large nails driven into the wall.

I also remember mother with a double-bladed ax in her hand, killing a three-foot long diamond-backed rattlesnake that had come too close to the house. It was in the wood pile. She heard its warning rattle when she went to get more fuel for the stove while she cooked supper one late afternoon. Mom was a courageous woman; it didn't occur to her to get Daddy to solve the problem. She simply dispatched the snake with a few well-placed strokes of the ax, and that was that. Doris and I were frightened, but awed. Had we been Nez Perce or Bannock children, after that incident we would probably have called her She Who Kills Rattlers!

We didn't see any more diamond-backs except that one, but we saw lots of small lizards sunning themselves on the rocks near the house. We watched the birds and insects, especially those near the small creek formed by run-off from the spring. We played a favorite game by the spring creek. We'd dam the rivulet, making a 'lake', around which we'd construct roads to and from an imaginary farm. We made farm-buildings from dried mud and built miniature rock fences.

Doris was only four, so the two of us often played school. Because I could write, I was the teacher, and I know she learned most of her ABCs from me. I often read to her and tried to teach her how to play card games. We'd visit Daddy at the mine, and later on, after his brothers, Cy and Uncle Joe had helped him build the forty-foot tower above the mine shaft, I was allowed to go to the bottom of the shaft one day, where two men were digging. Mom wasn't around or I probably wouldn't have been allowed to go.

Daddy let me wear his hard hat, which had a carbide light attached to the front, and I was just tall enough to be able to see over the edge of the big dump bucket. The round sides of the bucket came up to my chin and I held on tight to the edge. It was big enough to hold half a dozen children my size — with a bit of squeezing.

Slowly, I was lowered into the depths of the 150-foot shaft by means of a long half inch steel cable stretching up over a drum at the top of the tower, then down to another drum to which its end was fastened near the hoist. I smelled the wet earth and could see water oozing out of the sides of the shaft. Then, the bucket was steadied by the men as it approached bottom, and with a slight 'bump', I was in the center of the earth — or so it seemed to me.

Chet and Bill explained how they shoveled dirt and water into the bucket.

"We won't fill it up while you're in there!" they joked.

They wore fishing waders, because they were working in puddles of water about six inches deep. After they filled the bucket, they blew a whistle my dad had rigged on its big bail where the steel cable was attached. Then, Daddy would haul it "up top."

When the bucket came level with a sloping platform about twelve feet above the mouth of the shaft, it caught on a device he'd built that tipped the bucket almost upside down, causing the muddy earth and gravel to spill out and run down the platform into a small open railway car. Jack pushed the car the length of a two hundred foot narrow-gauge track leading to a shallow hillside where the unwanted earth was dumped by opening a trap on one end of the car.

I tingled and shivered with delight all the way down and all the way up the mine shaft, loving every minute of it in spite of the cold. The hoist engine sounded louder and louder as I reached the top of the shaft, just as its noise had gradually diminished during the descent. Daddy made the hoist, too, of course.

It was an old Ford truck engine mounted on four-by-four timbers, with a gear assembly attached permitting him to raise, lower, and dump the bucket over "the sump" — a large puddle of thick muddy water that accumulated just below the platform around the dumpster car.

When I'd returned to the earth's surface that day, he lifted me out of the bucket, laughing with me and matching my delight as I told him what I'd seen, felt and experienced. Then, he showed me how he operated the hoist, because in spite of the short interlude of my journey, he and his crew had to keep on working.

He explained how the hoist gears worked, shouting in my ear over the engine's clamor. I saw each operation of the gears as he carried them out, for he sat on a tractor seat so he could 'drive' the hoist with me on his lap.

From there, I could watch his beautiful strong hands manipulate the gears with coordinated precision and I could feel his hard chest and legs against my back. The smell of him enveloped me and I loved that too. He smelled of clean work shirt, tobacco, sweat, shaving cologne and diesel oil.

I loved my dad's hands and arms most of all because he handled everything he touched with assurance and care, whether it was his drum major's mace, the hoist gears, his daughters, the steering wheel of a car, dinner plates laden with good food, fishing rods, rifles, his necktie or his own face while he shaved it with an ivory-handled straight-razor.

That's why I was so terrified the night disaster struck at the mine. I was afraid he'd hurt — or lost — his hands.

Chapter 5

> Just when we're safe, there's a sunset-touch,
> A fancy from a flower-bell, someone's death,
> A chorus-ending from Euripides, —
> And that's enough for fifty hopes and fears
> As old and new at once as nature's self,
> To rap and knock and enter in our soul,
> Take hands and dance there, a fantastic ring,
> Round the ancient idol, on his base again, —
> The grand Perhaps.
>
> [*Bishop Blougram's Apology*, 1: 182,
> Robert Browning]

The hospital's corridors were white; the beds, ceilings, furniture and the nurses were white — bright with the illumination of electric lights, unmercifully revealing dirt and detail. Mom and I sat in the waiting room after she had driven to the Huntington Hospital in the truck with Jack's help.

By early evening, we arrived at the door of the Emergency Room, where doctors took over cleaning up the mess we brought — and my dad was a mess. How badly was he hurt? That was the silent question in our minds for several hours while the hospital staff worked on him. All we knew was that he'd had a freak accident. We didn't know how badly or permanently he was hurt.

There was a strong wind. When he carried a bucket of gasoline to fill the hoist's engine, a spark from his carbide light ignited the gas, which he threw away from him, but the bucket hit the engine at an angle throwing the burning gasoline back on his chest, arms and thighs. The gas tank of the hoist blew up. To make a long story short, he had third and fourth degree burns over most of the front of his body.

When we were allowed to see him, he lay perfectly still, swathed in wide white gauze, his lower body under a sheet-tent, arms supported on pillows at either side. All we could see of him, really, was his face, which had a couple of small bandages on it. The fire had singed his eyelashes and eyebrows and taken away the forelock of hair that often fell over his forehead, his face wasn't damaged. He'd torn off his hard-hat as soon as he got rid of the gas-bucket, then he ran, stumbling, for the sump. I was at the hospital because Mom wouldn't leave me alone at the Mormon Basin house. Doris was visiting Grammy and Granddad in Baker and was spared the fear at the hospital.

The events following Daddy's injury are largely unclear to me now. All I remember distinctly was the relief I felt when I found out that, in time, he would recover — that he wouldn't lose his hands. It took a long time for him to recuperate and he had scars on his arms, legs and chest for the rest of his life. His accident spelled the end of the mining venture in Mormon Basin.

Daddy worked in other mines though: copper mining in Rio Tinto, Nevada and gold mining in Cornucopia, Oregon, which is now a ghost town. My sister visited eastern Oregon recently. She tells me that the mountains are still as beautiful as they were, although now, only two buildings are still standing. The old road that led from the Coulter's lower entrance to the upper (Union) mine entrance can only be traveled on horseback or four-wheel drive truck.

Auntie Vi and Uncle Joe lived "up top," as the Union entrance was called. Distance-wise, their house was a little over a mile by winding, graded dirt road which ascended twelve hundred feet higher. During the winter, we children were allowed to attach our sled ropes to the huge diesel 'Cat' — the only vehicle that could make the ascent to the Union mine in winter when the snow was six to ten feet deep. The driver carried mail, packages, etc. to the people who lived near the Union, and I remember having hot cocoa and cookies at Auntie Vi's house before riding our sleds back down the winding road to the Coulter's entrance below.

Winters in Cornucopia were so beautiful! Snow completely covered our house and a few others situated in a hollow sheltered by the surrounding mountains away from the main road which led to the company store. Snow falls so differently in the mountains where there is little or no wind to drive it across flat land surfaces, as in the Great Plains. Snowflakes are huge in the mountains — so big that we could see their faint crystalline designs against the dark wool of our mittens and heavy coats. Everything gradually became blanketed in silence and mystery. The evergreen trees all looked like Christmas trees with their white-burdened branches and hanging icicles. Often, we couldn't get our front door fully open until Daddy squeezed out and shoveled more of the latest fall into what became a deep, roof-less, tunnel-entrance to the surface. People could ski over the roof of our house, but it was warm and snug inside.

My father was the AF of L (American Federation of Labor) steward at the Coulter in 1938-1940, and he taught first-aid classes every week to the men and their wives. I recall those classes as special occasions, for he often used me to demonstrate how to make leg, arm and neck splints, how to apply pressure to arteries to stop bleeding and the like. Those were the early days of the union movement in this country and men were preoccupied with "portal to portal pay" and better working conditions generally, especially in mines.

One of their rallying cries was "A fair day's work for a fair day's pay." My dad took his responsibilities seriously — so much so that he was instrumental finally in having the Coulter and the Union mines closed, never to re-open again. The mines were owned by Anaconda Copper, Inc., who only opened smaller mining operations when there was cheap labor: when they could hire men who would work under any conditions. Anaconda owned the whole town of Cornucopia; the general store, the service station — everything people had to depend upon for a living. Childlike, I didn't realize the significance of these things until much later, nor did I understand the additional importance of the first-aid classes, or that Daddy used these occasions not only to teach the men how to care for themselves and each other in cases of accident, but to teach them about their rights and obligations as workers.

In 1939-1940, union movements weren't yet rackets — at least not in the hinterlands of eastern Oregon. While we weren't entirely cut off from the rest of the world, from our vantage point in Cornucopia the world did seem far away. It's not surprising that Thornton Wilder's *Our Town* was the Pulitzer prize-winning drama in 1938, reflecting the localized ethos and isolationist mind-set of the majority of Americans. I remember my father mourning Feodor Chaliapin, who died that year, and Clarence Darrow, a lawyer whom he greatly admired. Because we had a radio, we knew President Roosevelt had recalled the American ambassador to Germany and there was no longer a German ambassador in Washington D.C. We knew too, in 1939, about the troubles in England — that women and children were evacuated from London, for example. We began to hear a lot about Winston Churchill, and Hitler's book, *Mein Kampf*, which was published the year the war started in Europe, although the U.S. was declared neutral.

It wasn't until 1940, however, when Congress passed the Selective Service Act, that it became clear to us that the United States would probably be in the war soon; the retreat from Dunkirk came as a shock, and the U.S. was trying to help England in every possible way. Daddy was upset because he knew he wouldn't be able to be a soldier again because of his age. He'd spent a lot of time in England during the first World War and loved it very much.

Although Calvin Coolidge won the Presidential election in 1924 and was still in office in 1928, the year I was born, Herbert Hoover was inaugurated President in 1929. Franklin Delano Roosevelt was inaugurated President in 1933, when Doris was born. By the time he was re-elected for the third term in 1940, I honestly didn't think there was (or ever would be) any other President!

I remember, too, that my favorite popular song was *September Song*, which came out in 1938. *Harbor Lights* (a hit song in 1937) always made Auntie Violet cry because it reminded her of Alaska. Kate Smith sang *God Bless America*, popular in 1939, which was my mother's favorite. By the time 1941 came we had moved to Redding, California. People were singing *Bewitched, Bothered and Bewildered*, *Deep in the Heart of Texas* and *I Don't Want to Set the World on Fire*, but we did, starting in December, when the Pacific war started.

In those days I had to come straight home from school because I looked after Doris until Mom and Daddy got home at six or six-thirty. Turning on the radio I heard the news on December eighth about the attack on Pearl Harbor. What it meant to the eighth grader I was at the time was simply the fact that we wouldn't now be able to go to Hawaii, where my dad had signed on for a big construction job which was meant to start in January 1942, at Pearl Harbor. That's really all the declaration of war meant to me until many months later when I was enrolled in Jefferson High School as a freshman. My parents were among the many who flocked to Portland, Oregon where the shipyards provided the main job attraction to many people from all over the country, some of whom had surely moved around as much as we did between 1936 and 1941.

There was Sumpter where we lived in two converted railway cars in a picturesque wooded dell with a spring and a creek nearby; Mormon Basin, where we carried water and lived in a millboard shack; Rio Tinto, Spirit Lake, and Cornucopia, where we occupied 'company houses'; finally to Redding, where we rented a house, because by that time, Daddy was making much more money. The United States had begun to emerge from the Depression in 1937-38 owing to the European war. Between 1936 and 1941, we had to move to places where my father could find work, but I've never been sorry about that, partly because in two of those small towns, Sumpter and Cornucopia, I was lucky enough to be able to attend a one-room schoolhouse. Maybe that's why I'm still fond of the television series *Little House on the Prairie*. The houses we lived in weren't situated on prairies — even the sagebrush desert that surrounded Mormon Basin was in higher altitudes. Baker City itself is located in the high Columbia Plateau country of eastern Oregon, surrounded by snow-covered mountains.

It isn't the physical landscape of *Little House* that I find appealing, but the schoolhouse and the memories of the kind of education I received in similar buildings. I'm told that what I describe sounds almost impossible to friends who were stuck in large, urban public school settings, where they learned very quickly to become digits in a system. My sister, I'm sure, didn't fare as well as I did, although she, too, was in the adjoining classroom in Cornucopia, which had a two-room schoolhouse; one room for grades one through four, the other for grades five through eight.

Originally, it was thanks to the Franciscan sisters in Baker at St. Francis Academy that I learned to read and write, although I could count to a thousand, say the ABCs, and recognize many words when I started first grade. Everyone learned 'phonics' when I began, and many also learned Palmer penmanship. There simply wasn't any other way to learn to read. Doris wasn't so lucky. By the time she started primary school, somebody somewhere had decided that the phonic method was "old-fashioned" with the result that my sister never learned to read properly. Years later she took remedial courses in order to cope and that helped a lot, but the worst part was that she never *enjoyed* reading as I did. Basically, she was never really taught how to read so she could figure out new words by herself. I'm convinced that anyone who hasn't learned phonics hasn't learned how to read. Then, too, I find it amusing nowadays to see so many people "hooked on phonics." They seem amazed that their children learn so well and that the learning sticks. They may or may not know that the basics of the method aren't "new." It's how everyone learned in 1935, and it's because of being able to read and write very well that I excelled in one-room schoolhouse situations. There, if you could finish the work your grade was doing, you were permitted to move on. I read fourth and fifth grade books the whole time I was in third grade in Sumpter, and I was reading at seventh and eighth grade levels while I was in fifth and sixth grades in Cornucopia.

I can't ever remember not wanting to read. That's why the old brown dictionary went everywhere with me when I was little and why it ranked first over any of the toys I possessed. Not only did I love reading in school, I spent marvelous hours at the Baker Public Library during all the periods, long or short, that I stayed with Grammy and Granddad. Picking gooseberries was only one of many things I did. The Baker Library, like most of its kind throughout the United States, was a Carnegie Library. Much later, after I'd finished a Doctoral degree in social anthropology, while studying for a Master's degree in Library Science from Indiana University (1984-85), I wrote an essay praising the virtues of the Scots immigrant who became an American industrialist. Whatever else he may have done, Andrew Carnegie blessed his adopted country with libraries.

I still have clear memories of pausing before I pushed the heavy glass door which opened into the basement where the junior library was housed. I always paused, both to savor the anticipated fragrance of the place and thoughts of the books I knew would conduct me to other worlds. After pausing, I opened the door and stood inside enchanted, as I slowly looked around the huge room lined with its treasure of hundreds of books. I continued my private ritual after I'd read my way through the junior library and was allowed to take books from the senior library upstairs. I earned the name 'bookworm' at an early age!

"You can always find Shirley" Grandpa would say, "because she'll be somewhere with her nose in a book."

When the weather was inclement, he meant I could probably be found curled up on the davenport in the living room. When the weather was fine during the long days of spring, summer and fall, he expected to find me firmly ensconced in the Y-shaped branches of an apple tree located between the hen house and the barn, some distance from the door of Grammy's big kitchen. I'd rigged up a shelf where I put the books I wasn't reading, arranging an old pillow against which I leaned, supported by the main trunk of tree.

The vista provided by the improvised balcony seat in the apple tree was splendid. Grandpa's farm was situated on the south side of town, so, apart from some farm buildings on land which was over a mile away, Baker valley stretched uninterrupted before my eyes to the foothills of the Blue Mountains on my right and the Wallowas on the left. Big Lookout and Bald Mountain were prominent features of the landscape. Their aspect, like the view itself, was never the same, depending upon weather conditions even on clear days.

I think it was Christmas, 1935 or 1936 that I found a bicycle under the tree with my name on it. I suspect the Chandler side of the family had contributed to its purchase because not much else had my name on it that year. I was ecstatic. The bike was a red and silver Schwinn. Best of all, it was brand new and it was mine. It didn't take long for Daddy to teach me to ride it, thus increasing my range of mobility. The bike was fitted with a carrier on its back fender that would carry a dozen or so books depending on their size. I tooled back and forth from Grammy's farm to music lessons and the library on the north side of town, carrying the load of cherished books with me.

Although I read a lot, it wasn't the only thing I did with Grammy. She had vegetables in her big garden at the side of the house, and flower plots were situated in both front and back yards where she grew pansies, "bleeding hearts" (a kind of fuchsia), peonies, gladiolas, iris (we called them "flags"), marigolds, zinnias, dahlias, bachelor buttons, baby breath, daffodils and other kinds of flowers. It was from her that I learned how to plant and care for flowers, herbs and vines.

"Shirley, you put your book down now and help me in the garden" she'd say. "My stars, child, you'll grow onto that davenport, you've been there so long." Laughing, I'd tear myself away to help her plant, weed and hoe whatever she was growing. Perhaps she needed the chicken that Granddad had killed that morning picked and cleaned. Maybe she wanted eggs from the hen house or the butter needed churning. If it was summertime, I'd take iced tea or lemonade to Granddad and the man who helped him at the gravel plant which he owned that occupied the land northwest of the farm.

Granddad was a man of few words, but he was kind and observing. He taught me how to play checkers and cribbage; his two favorite games. We'd play in the evenings after supper, and I'm sure he let me win enough times so that I didn't get discouraged. I never heard Grandpa utter a swearword, in contrast to Uncle Raleigh, who swore all the time. The worst thing Granddad could say about someone was that he or she was "a silly fool."

Maybe it was the library and reading that shielded me from thinking my sister and I were what is now called "deprived" in any way. We must have appeared economically "disadvantaged" to some people, even in those days. But, social engineering hadn't reached the proportions all over the country that it has now — and probably had in large cities even then.

Doris and I didn't grow up with television, thus we weren't constantly bombarded with advertising, nor did we develop unnaturally short attention-spans. I didn't grow up thinking I was special because my parents didn't have much money, nor, intellectually, did I mature thinking there was all that 'stuff' out there that I had to have to be happy or to get on in the world. True, there were lots of kids who had more clothes and toys than I did and finer places to live, but to me that wasn't what was important. None of my friends seemed to be any happier or any smarter than my sister and I were, nor did they have any more fun.

Mom never let a birthday go by without baking and decorating a cake and organizing some kind of little party. I often awakened when I was small to find an Easter basket or Valentine's Day present beside my pillow. Sometimes the presents my sister and I received were homemade, and sometimes our Christmas stockings had more apples, oranges and nuts in them than toys, but that didn't matter. To this day, I enjoy making Christmas decorations out of colored "construction paper" as we called it, pasting circles made from paper into chains and stringing popcorn and cranberries. We always had a special star for the top of the tree and Mom had salvaged strings of lights, tinfoil icicles and some glass ornaments from the things she'd once had. It was the lights that made everything so beautiful anyway, even though we couldn't have them in Mormon Basin or Sumpter because there was no electricity. We always visited Grammy and Granddad at Christmas and they had electric lights on their tree. Anyway, the highlight of Christmas was Midnight Mass and the splendor of the lavishly decorated church — an event I looked forward to every year.

No one went to Midnight Mass on Christmas eve, 1946, when Daddy was sentenced to life in the State prison in Salem. There were no Christmas presents — only family members crying, looking grim or, like Nana, having hysterics. They all said we should be glad he hadn't been sent to the gas chamber.

I got away from them by retreating upstairs and reading books. The only emotion I felt was disgust over the way the trial had gone. I blamed the Bowden side of the family for that. They didn't know what was going on, and to my severe teen-ager's standards, the family didn't know what they were doing. They trusted Daddy's lawyer. I didn't.

Three years later, my lack of trust in Patterson was vindicated, although I didn't know I'd been right about him until 1995, when I came across an article from the *Oregon Journal* (Tuesday, January 25, 1949). The article announces J. Robert Patterson's permanent disbarment from practice in the United States district court of Oregon for "flagrant disregard of rules governing professional conduct of lawyers." Among the improprieties listed, it was said, "That it was "improper" to represent J. Westley Bowden in defending a murder charge in the circuit court of the state of Oregon." I still think Daddy's trial lawyers believed he was guilty. The problem for me at the time was that the family let circumstances and the lawyers dictate to them, instead of taking charge of the situation themselves.

Compassion is an adult emotion. Working with Dr. Wadro fifteen years later, I finally understood why some members of the Bowden side of the family behaved as they did. I forgave them, but I also found out why I didn't follow their pattern. Part of it was a rebellion against my mother which emerged full force during my teen-age years. To me, Fern Bowden became a symbol of everything I didn't want to be.

Chapter 6

> Footfalls echo in the memory
> Down the passage we did not take
> Towards the door we never opened
> Into the rose-garden. My words echo
> Thus, in your mind.
>   Humankind
> cannot bear very much reality.
>
> [*Four Quartets. Burnt Norton I.* T.S. Eliot]

Wes Bowden was no paragon of virtue by anyone's standards, but until I was a sophomore in high school and because we'd been so close, he was to me. At some very fundamental level, he trusted me — which Mom never did. Nor did he whip me, which Mom often did, no doubt getting rid of some of the frustrations and dissatisfaction she felt about her own life in that way.

I'll never forget the last time she took a stick to me over some infraction of the many rules she made in her efforts to gain control. I don't recall what caused her fury one of the last times she flew at me, except that it had to do with dancing. I do remember not crying or reacting on that occasion — I'd decided on that after the last time it happened. I simply stood there until she finally quit. My bottom and the backs of my legs were still sore an hour or two later. She never beat me again after that. I was fifteen. My impassive silent response to her fury had some positive effects, especially, I think, on my sister, who if anything, suffered more than I did from these scenes — and 'scenes' they were — acted out in unconscious response to some unwritten, unvoiced script that dominated her life. My one regret regarding my mother is that she didn't live long enough for us to be reconciled — for me to find out what drove her to the kinds of unlovable, bitchy things she did, not only to me but to others. Privately, among family members, my mother wasn't seen as a lovable woman. Efficient? yes; knowledgeable, gracious, and strong? yes; but likable — no. She was, however, publicly well-liked.

Years later, I tried to find out from her mother and from members of both sides of the family what her problems were, but in death, as in life, she remained mysteriously enshrined in an aura of goodness that was, for all practical purposes, indestructible. Daddy refused to listen to anything negative or critical about her up to the end, and he wasn't alone — no one wanted to hear about her faults. It was as if she had none. I've always wondered if that wasn't her problem. She was consistently deferred to and invariably protected, not only from external criticism, but from self-criticism. Her wishes took precedence over anyone else's who happened to be around. Not only my father treated her this way, members of his family, as well as her own did too. I think Mom grew up and lived most of her adult life sincerely believing she could do no real wrong — a myth she understandably nourished as it developed. Comprehensible though the myth was however, it proved to be her downfall — and Daddy's.

I've conjectured, too, about the pedestal he put her on. To him, Mom was the embodiment of all that was good: all that was womanly and admirable. She was, as he never tired of telling us, "the finest woman in the world." She'd had more schooling than he had. She finished high school. But he, the oldest of six children, was never able to go to school beyond eighth grade because he had to work. After 1906 he was the main support of his mother, three brothers and two sisters.

My paternal grandfather, James Herron Bowden, like his father before him, was a colorful character, but he was rarely ever around their Jordan Valley ranch. His wife, whom we called 'Nan' or 'Nana' was barely 15 years old when she gave birth to Wes — her first child — thus it's not surprising that she and the younger children depended upon him. Whatever my father had, or knew, he learned for himself. He was a self-made man, which has both positive and negative aspects. On the one hand, he managed to craft a life for himself and his family that was much better than that of a typical ranch hand, a 'buckaroo', which was where he started. On the other, he possessed all of the bigotry, prejudices and self-congratulating complacency typical of self-made men, regardless of economic background.

According to standards of the time, Mom and her brother, my Uncle Marion, were much better off. Marion completed a B.A. degree in business administration from Oregon State College and Fern completed high school as an average student, then went to business college. Their parents, like theirs before them, were "the salt of the earth" — considerably more stable in many ways than the Bowden side of the family. Fern Chandler's completely different life-style was probably part of what attracted Wes to her. The Chandlers were Protestants (Baptists). The Bowdens were Catholics (and not very good ones at that!).

Without exception, the Chandlers were models of middle-class American values: farmers, shopkeepers and small businessmen. Great Grandpa Bowden was an *entrepreneur*, a cattle rancher and landowner. John Baptist Bowden is still revered in Oregon history books for his role in the development of eastern Oregon's Jordan Valley and for his part in the history of the Wells-Fargo Company. By the time Wes came along, however, the ranch had fallen on hard times. John's son, James, wasn't the manager his father had been.

Mom was, I think, both symbol and embodiment of a life my father never had. He was one of the most handsome and eligible bachelors in Baker before and after the first World War. He was a romantic and dashing figure very different from the other men with whom she was acquainted. Whatever they may have thought of each other, a more unfortunate combination of personalities, symbols and background could hardly be imagined.

They were married five days before mother's twenty-seventh birthday, November seventh, 1926, after a long engagement. They went to Seattle by train for their honeymoon, but I've always suspected that the honeymoon was quickly over, given the sexual mores of the time and given that, to my mother (and her mother), sex was something to be endured, not enjoyed. That's not speculation: both women later told me how they felt.

Maybe my parents enjoyed having sex with one another, but I doubt it. They never seemed to be a couple in that way.

They weren't demonstrative in front of "the children." If they were deeply in love, they managed effectively to hide it. If they did fulfill each other's sexuality, lives and dreams, it wasn't discernible — not in the ways I've known other couples to act who were personally fulfilled in that way. My parents lived in the same house, ate from the same table and went many places together, but they remain irrevocably divided in my perception. In some strange way, it is as if they had never been married. I still find their mutual attraction hard to understand, because, as far as I could (or can) see, they had very little in common.

I've lived with photographs of their courtship days for years, for example. But even in these, they seem to be 'posing' for the person behind the camera, or for the group of young people they ran around with on camping trips, picnics, etc. They rarely agreed about anything, whether it was my sister's and my behavior, or, what was good to be or to do. They never agreed about where they should go on an outing, or what to eat when they were in a restaurant.

Like all of the Chandlers, Mom was a teetotaler. She wouldn't touch a drop of anything alcoholic. My father drank (occasionally too much for his own or anyone else's good, I admit) and he insisted that my sister and I learn to drink at home. When company came, we were given tumblers full of gingerale, but these were "highballs, just like the grown-ups" because he added a tablespoon full of bourbon or gin.

"If they're not curious about it — if they can have drinks at home, they won't sneak around" Daddy would say. And he was right. Both Doris and I found the clandestine drinking of high-school friends boring, because to us, alcoholic drinks were neither exciting nor "new." They weren't forbidden, which was the main reason our classmates went through elaborate schemes and concocted cover stories concealing their pathetic attempts to discover what the fuss was all about.

High schools had sororities and fraternities in those days and I remember being invited to join one of them during my senior year. Curious, I went to the chaperoned social gathering that was held one evening in a public building near the school for the purpose of looking over prospective members. The occasion was called a 'smoker'. I remember complaining bitterly to Mom that my clothes weren't right for the occasion. I knew I wouldn't be dressed properly for the part I'd be expected to play. Although I had black and white saddle shoes, white anklets and pleated skirts, none of the skirts were pastel-plaid or made from real wool. The skirt I wore that night was navy-blue, made from some other kind of material. I wore a short-sleeved sweater and cardigan but it wasn't a cashmere sweater-set like the other girls had. Instead of a single string of pearls, I wore a delicate gold chain with a locket and bracelet to match. I did have a watch, but it was one of Mom's and it had a thin black strap instead of a gold or silver stretch-band — another requirement for the high-school girl's 'uniform' back then — nor did I wear lipstick.

None of my girlfriends, especially Katherine Ware, Patty Wittman and Jean Anderson wore lipstick, although most of the girls I was acquainted with did. Kate and Patty were fellow members of the International Club and the Library Guild — groups that I enjoyed immensely. My boyfriends were chosen from these groups too: I remember Keith Timmens (a budding lawyer), Don Webber (an artist) and Charles Cartwright (an aspiring drama director).

More important, they were honors students. Katie eventually taught Mediæval English at Stanford University and Patty became a Carmelite nun. Frank Bowman (also on the honor roll), did his graduate work in literature at the Sorbonne. I made the honor roll too, but only just. Unlike my friends, I was at the bottom, not the top of the list.

Jean Anderson wasn't an honors student, but she was an excellent ballet dancer. We shared lessons at R.D. Dare's School of Dancing which formed the basis for another life after school at least four evenings per week and Saturdays. The dance studio was of great interest to me. Because of my inner circle of friends and the activities we shared, I found the social affairs of the sorority who "rushed" me in 1945 very dull.

Prospective members were greeted at the door by its officers and both male and female chaperones because it was an affair jointly sponsored by one of the fraternities (whose name also escapes me). We were ushered into a big dimly-lit room meant to resemble a cabaret. Card tables with lighted candles and red-checked tablecloths were arranged informally around a dance floor presided over by a quintet of musicians which included two vocalists.

I liked dancing, but was used to dancing with people who were very good at it. One of my partners at the smoker that night said, "Gee, if I'd known you were such a good dancer, I'd never have asked you." Accustomed to having wine at evening meals with my father if I wanted it, and cocktails when my parents' friends visited, I wasn't thrilled by having beer and cigarettes on this occasion. Having exhausted comments about the weather, comparisons of football, basketball or baseball teams and games, a few rather inept sexual innuendoes and gossip about absent acquaintances (which I naively thought was a prelude to real conversation still to come), nothing else developed. I quickly discovered that any mention of books, plays, international affairs, art, music or ideas were outside the pale in this group, excepting two of the chaperones, who informed me I wasn't there to talk to them, but to "people my own age." However, no one my own age with whom I relished talking was there.

Looking back, I'm sure my conversational gambits were as boring to members of my host groups as theirs were to me. I couldn't have cared less who won the last football game, which team might win the next one or who would be elected prom queen and king. I wasn't interested in who was dating whom, the latest hair styles and fashions. I wanted to have the right 'costume' for any occasion, but I didn't want to dress the same way the sorority crowd did all the time.

At the smoker, I became aware for the first time of how my real friends and I were classified by this group. We were socially marginalized by the sorority/fraternity crowd. I didn't fully realize that studying dancing as a hobby or taking classes as a substitute physical exercise was 'OK' to these people, but professional dancing of any kind wasn't on the list of socially acceptable occupations. I hadn't a clue, either, about the enormous price extracted from those who are different by adult versions of that group of teen-agers, nor was I conscious of how superior my friends and I felt in relation to them.[1] After all, we were the real leaders in the school and we were smarter than they were, weren't we? I justify making a point of my first conscious contact with the mainstream America of the mid-'forties because for the first time at the sorority party, I became keenly aware of outside pressures to conform. Up to then, conformity meant family. The outside world meant freedom.

Teenager that I was, I learned more about what I was *not* from the experience than what sort of human being I *was*. The perceptions thus gained were to prove valuable through the ordeal to come. I talked with some of my friends at length: "I'm not boy-crazy, am I Katie? There's nothing wrong with me because I don't like football games? It's what's inside of a person that counts, isn't it?"

"Don't worry about it" Katie said, "they don't know what they're missing. You wouldn't give up anything you have for what they think is important, would you?"

"No, I wouldn't. I won't give up dancing for anything and I'd have been better off reading a book than wasting my time listening to their chatter — that's for sure." Fortunately, I could excuse myself from sorority membership gracefully, as I was able to graduate from high school early. The class with whom I entered graduated in June, 1946, but I left Jefferson High behind me in January that year.

Throughout this period, I have very little recollection of relating to my sister, except that we shared a bedroom at home. I knew she was struggling with being a high-school freshman and she was convinced that I was "stuck-up." Unlike me, Doris wanted very much to be with her highschool "in-group." She went to the games, wanted to be a cheer-leader and she let me know she thought the ballet dancing, classical music and the talking I did (that she didn't understand) was "dumb." Not only that, the inter-

---

[1] I think very few people transcend their teen-aged classifications of others and general social outlook. Dancing was a marginal occupation in America in those days; perhaps it still is. The marginalization was real: for example, I had no social security and couldn't get a bank loan when I had a studio in New York City.

minable arguments between our parents had started, splitting the family between Mom and Doris on one side and Dad and me on the other. The fighting over what had happened to the money my father sent home from Adak began almost immediately after he returned from Alaska in November 1945.

Mom's utilitarian views about books were a major source of bitter altercation between her and me. Recipe books were all right because reading them produced tangible results. The books she'd used to learn shorthand, typing and business practices were practical, thus time spent reading them wasn't wasted. She liked a few magazines. I remember *Good Housekeeping*, *Cosmopolitan* and *Reader's Digest* being high on her priority list because they contained useful information and had entertaining articles in them — but history books? What was the sense of knowing a lot of useless things about the past of people and countries nobody ever heard of?

Philosophy? Now that was a real waste of time! Why fill your head with a bunch of silly ideas and spend time talking about things that didn't make any difference in the real world anyway?

Literature? Well, she supposed there might be some good in that, but people would be better off reading the Bible. As for fairy tales, ballets and plays; all they deserved was a derisive snort, usually accompanied by a derogatory remark about Daddy's love for such things. "Where" she wanted to know, "had Opera, Plato and high-falutin' talk ever got him?"

One of the last couple of beatings I took was over dancing. All I remember about the dissension that led up to it was her statement, "I'd rather you be a prostitute than a dancer." I was a cheeky kid, telling her in no uncertain terms she ought to be glad I wanted to be a dancer — and then the fun began.

My sister dreaded the frequent quarrels Mom and I had. She was always nervous and apprehensive when the three of us were home alone. Years later, she told me she eventually came to harbor intense dislike for both of us because we caused her so much pain. She saw the injustice in most of Mom's attacks on me, but she identified so closely with her that she felt disloyal and guilty if she didn't agree with everything she said and did.

The dancing was the main source of contention: the time I spent at the studio, the way it affected (in her words) "how I behaved" — everything. It was only because of our family doctor that I was able to take lessons. Soon after arriving in Portland, Mom took me to Dr. Taylor because she thought something was the matter with me, as I didn't want to attend family picnics, go to movies, etc. I was twelve.

Finishing the physical examination, Doctor Taylor said, "Shirley, there's nothing the matter with you that I can see. What's wrong? Is there something you really want to do?"

"Take ballet lessons" I instantly replied.

"And why don't you?" he asked.

"Because Mom won't let me. She thinks dancing is evil."

"I see" he said. "Now don't you say anything about this talk we've had, and I'll see what I can do."

Mystified, I finished dressing and went from examining room into his office in time to hear him telling mother that I was to take one of the pills he gave her in a large bottle every day (I'm sure they were placebos). He then wrote a prescription which stated I was to take two ballet lessons per week because I wasn't getting the "right kind" of exercise. Mom couldn't argue with medical authority although she grumbled about the prescription all the way home.

Once started, I never looked back. Mom would only pay for two classes per week so I found a job in the corner drugstore jerking sodas to pay for additional lessons. Later on, I bargained with Mr. Dare for cleaning the studio in exchange for lessons and soon, I was taking ten classes per week. Three months later when Mother and I were back in Dr. Taylor's office for my check-up, he pronounced me 'well', but insisted I continue with dancing, emphasizing that the special exercise was necessary for my health. I thanked him many times for "our little secret," as he called it, because I knew very well what he had done.

When I finished high school, I got a job at the Portland Art Museum as an artist's model for a dollar fifty per hour (friends who worked in department stores only made ninety cents). Mom was furious. She couldn't believe I'd "stand naked in front of all those people."[2] This time, Daddy defended me, as he had gone to the Museum and inquired about the job. He talked at length to me about it and I don't think she ever forgave him for that. He said, "Fern, she'll be seventeen in October. If she doesn't know the difference between right and wrong by now, she never will no matter what she does. It isn't the job but how she handles it that counts." To me, that was further proof of my father's trust. Simultaneously, the issue illustrated how ashamed of me my mother was. She asked many times, "What will I say to people about it?"

"Tell them she's making good money doing something she likes" he said. "She's learning a lot about art at the Museum. Besides, she'll be going to college in the fall so you won't have to worry about the modeling. Leave her alone, Fern, you can't run her life."

During the last months before Mom died in 1946, our family was a pressure-cooker of tensions fired by the heat of struggles for control; but I learned something from the power-games my parents played.

Three years later I had a choice to make. Would I be a victim of circumstance or take charge of my own life?

---

[2] Clothed models only made $1.10 per hour. Nude models made $1.50.

Chapter 7

> From wrong to wrong the exasperated spirit
> Proceeds, unless restored by the refining fire
> Where you must move in measure, like a dancer.
>
> [T.S. Eliot -*Little Gidding, 2*]

It was November twenty-seventh, 1949, six weeks after my twenty-first birthday. I was married again, having met my second husband at the Arthur Murray Studio in Portland, where we both worked until we were able to open our own business. We enjoyed a leisurely breakfast, then Dorian went to the corner store to purchase a Sunday newspaper. Both of us relished anything that didn't require physical exertion. We had enough of that during the week, given rehearsals, classes, etc. at the successful dance studio we maintained in Portland, called *Rehearsal House*.

We needed rest from our activities the night before — a weekly Saturday engagement at a friend's nightclub, *El Rancho Village* on the outskirts of the city. We performed at a champagne-hour from six to seven o'clock, staying on until ten, offering free trial dancing lessons to patrons of the club, organizing 'mixer' dances, etc.

Apart from rehearsals and the exhibition dances we did, teaching a few classes and the task of bookkeeping for the business, Dorian audited courses in Theater Arts at Portland State College while I taught a weekly regimen of ballet classes and private lessons. That Sunday, we'd planned a short drive and an early dinner in the country, followed by an evening of playing cards with newly-married friends from Reed College. Those plans never materialized.

After looking through several sections of the newspaper in companionable silence for half an hour, I noticed Dorian wasn't reading anymore. Instead, he sat very still, gazing at me intently — so much so, I said, "What's the matter, honey? Have I got egg on my face, is my lipstick on crooked or something?"

"I wish it *were* something like that," he replied.

"Well, what's the matter with you, then?"

Almost imperceptibly straightening his shoulders, he got up from his armchair. Carrying part of the newspaper, he came to the dining room table, sitting across from me.

"I'd better tell you about this and read it with you so you won't find out about it from someone else."

"Tell me about what?" I asked, sensing his disquiet but unaware of its source.

"When does your dad come up for parole?" he asked.

"Sometime in 1954, I think. Why?"

"Well, I'm afraid the newspapers are going to make trouble for you and your sister again" he said. "There's no easy way to break it to you. Look at this." Opening the *American Weekly* section of *The Oregonian*, he laid it across the table.

A banner headline, accompanied by a mediocre drawing of a youngish-looking woman kneeling in front of a trunk, her hands on its lock, clamored for attention: **THE PANDORA BOX MURDER**, the hateful headline announced, amplified by inset photographs of the "slayer," sub-titles, etc.

"Oh my God!" I said softly. "What's this all about?"

"Your mother and father, you, and your sister."

My eyes filled with tears. "Why won't they leave him alone? Why won't they leave *us* alone?"

Dorian moved his chair so that he sat beside me. We looked at the spectacle of the double-page spread (continued on a third page) together, his left arm around my shoulders.

Then, with his right hand under my chin, he forced me to look at him. He spoke slowly and with careful emphasis:

"Listen to me, my darling" he said, "This is the way the world works. Lots of people out there don't understand your dad's case the way you do. As far as they're concerned, your dad committed a murder. He's in prison. The case is on public record, therefore, he's fair game. Unfortunately, even though you and your sister had nothing to do with what your parents did to themselves, you're fair game too. And that's not all. I've seen it happen before. When someone is convicted of a capital crime, no matter what the circumstances, if the verdict is 'guilty' the person's story is continually dredged up, sensationalized and brought to public attention. Sometimes, that's a good thing, but sometimes it isn't. In your dad's case, it isn't — it's just a damned shame." He paused while I wiped my wet face, concluding helplessly,

"I don't know what else to say to you."

As he talked, part of my mind focused on what he was saying, but part of it darted around among the possible consequences of my suddenly reaffirmed notoriety, mainly its possible effects on our business. I taught many children's classes. Shuddering inside, I wondered if people would start treating me like Typhoid Mary again.

I thought about Daddy's shattered hopes for parole. He kept himself going in virtue of the belief that society would somehow be satisfied with the price it had extracted for the debt he owed and let him go when the appointed seven years were up. Every time I visited him at the penitentiary in Salem, he talked about paying his debt, telling me that seven years wasn't so long and not to worry — nor did I.

By 1949, he had become a trustee. According to Warden George Alexander, he was a model prisoner. He was allowed to have the record player and records I bought for him in his cell, and he had plenty of books, which he loved. He never complained that any injustice had been done to him. His main concern was for my sister and me — whether we were tormented in any way because of his situation. He would suffer on our behalf because of this damnable journalistic rehash — as if he hadn't suffered enough already!

Even when I talked to him about the possibility of reopening his case, he reminded me of the impossibility of presenting new evidence, since he'd been convicted on circumstantial evidence in the first place. He believed it would be "merely a matter of our word against theirs" — and it had already been decided that his word wasn't good enough. Moreover, he didn't seem to think that his lawyer viewed appealing the decision with favor. Rather, Mr. Patterson kept emphasizing how lucky he was not to have got a death sentence and Daddy bought into these definitions and assessments of his life. He was comforted by my desire to reopen his case, but he wasn't optimistic. "Better to wait for parole" summed up his attitude.

Dorian and I read through the libellous article, which started with misinformation about the trunk (actually, a footlocker), saying that it had been wired to explode when my mother opened it. My sister and I were mentioned by name several times, the author making much out of what he considered the fact that we could have opened the trunk after having been warned by Daddy not to do so. As I read through column after misrepresented column of the sordid, pitiful story, the old familiar rage I'd lived with since July 1946 was aroused full force. My father may not have thought injustice was done, but I did.

Following several interviews, early the next year (1950), I found a young lawyer, Bob Jordan, who said he would take the case on a contingency basis — half of whatever judgment was awarded, whether it was something or nothing. He didn't extend much hope of winning, largely because there hadn't yet been a case of invasion of personal privacy tried in the state of Oregon. Such complaints were without precedent. He would have to depend on precedents established in other states, notably Pennsylvania.

I think this is why Jordan took my case: no matter what happened, his reputation as a lawyer would be greatly enhanced. He faced going through a long process consuming many months, during which he appeared in hearings before six judges, but in the end, a decision was taken that my case would be tried before a jury.

When the trial started in October 1953, it lasted the better part of a week, including the pre-trial jury selection which I attended. I appeared at the trial alone, except for Bob Jordan. Doris and her husband were living in Seneca, Oregon, near the town of John Day. She couldn't come to Portland at the time. Aunt Margaret and her children weren't interested in having anything to do with the affair, largely because Helen was teaching at Jefferson High School. Margaret didn't want her daughter's life or her reputation besmirched by connections with me or the events that had taken place in 1946. Uncle Stan and Aunt Hazel were in Bend, and Phil and Etta lived in California.

I mention the lack of Bowden family support for two reasons: by the time my case came to trial, I'd given up serious attempts to relate to that side of the family. My life-style was too different, and, as far as I knew, they couldn't cope with it. I had long since concluded that there was no point trying to depend upon them for anything. Thus, a pattern formed that continues throughout my life: whenever significant events occur that touch me profoundly, I am alone. Even Dorian, who was completely supportive at home, didn't come to court with me. He said he shouldn't come to the trial because I needed to go through the ordeal by myself, so I did.

I felt bad about being alone during the trial: it was attached in my mind to being the 'black sheep' of the family — the outcast. The case was opposed, but mainly ignored, by the Chandler side of the family. In spite of hating my father, Grammy always welcomed me. We got along because we didn't talk about my father or "the incident." They all knew, however, that in the end, I was fighting the case against *The American Weekly* for my father, and its effects were far-reaching.

A two-hundred-fourteen word article appeared on a back page of *The Oregonian* in 1953, the text of which I reproduce to illustrate how, in spite of the evidence Jordan and I produced, news reporters *still* managed to get things wrong.

$850 Awarded In News Case
Published Article Basis of Action

A suit by Shirley Bowden against the Oregonian Publishing Company for $50,000 charging invasion of the right of privacy was decided Monday in favor of the plaintiff, who was awarded $850. The trial was in the court of Circuit Judge Martin Hawkins.

The basis of the suit was an article published in the *American Weekly* magazine section and distributed in The Sunday *Oregonian* November 27, 1949. The article described the murder of Mrs.

Wes Bowden of Portland, whose husband was convicted of first-degree murder by a jury in 1946. Shirley Bowden is the eldest daughter of Mr. and Mrs. Wes Bowden.

Dynamite in Locker

Mrs. Wes Bowden was killed by the blast of six sticks of dynamite which exploded when she opened her husband's foot locker. The story described the events before the murder and during the trial.

In the suit, the plaintiff claimed mental anguish because the American Weekly published the story three years after the murder and trial took place. The defendant contended right of privacy had not been invaded because the article substantially narrated matters of public record.

J. Robert Jordan represented the plaintiff and George Black Jr. and David Fain, of Black, Kendall and Fain, represented the defense.

The best part was the ethical and moral victory Jordan and I achieved. *The American Weekly's* format had to be changed. I received a written vote of thanks from many of the inmates of the Oregon State Penitentiary because of it. My dad's calamity wasn't the only lurid, sensationalized account of people's misfortune that appeared week after week in its pages. The format and content of the publication was the lowest form of tabloid journalism imaginable, based on rehashes of human catastrophe. Any rational person would agree that change could only be an improvement.

As it later turned out, Dorian's and my business wasn't adversely affected by the trial, largely because very few people connected with our studio knew who Shirley Bowden was. To them, I was Drid Williams professionally, and Mrs. Dorian Ross otherwise. Fortunately, most people's memories are short and notoriously vague.

However, the memory games I'd played and the double consciousness paid off at the trial. Even though a Portland firm of lawyers represented the Chicago-based newspaper corporation, Hearst sent two lawyers to Portland to augment the Portland firm's team for the trial. They were aggressive in their attempts to discredit my testimony, repeatedly trying to catch me out by quoting Doris's and other family members' statements. They would, for example, begin their questions with "You said your father told you not to go into the basement. Doesn't that mean he had prior knowledge of what could happen?" I contradicted them — as I had contradicted the Portland police in 1946 — telling them exactly what I did say. They tried to give the impression that I didn't love my father and hadn't visited him in prison, which was a lie. According to Mr. Jordan, they tried "every trick in the book" but none of it worked. The jury voted in my favor and I was ecstatic.

Because Daddy came up for parole the first time in 1954, I felt he now had a better chance of a positive outcome at his first parole hearing. I was seriously committed to the idea of reopening his case. Several things had emerged at my trial that pointed to prosecution weaknesses at his trial, including perjury on the part of some of their witnesses. There could no longer be any doubt that he was convicted solely on circumstantial evidence.

In the meantime, professional interests intervened. Four of my students and I were invited to London to Sadler's Wells School to study ballet. I was torn between the desire to go to England and my responsibility to Daddy, who encouraged me to go. By this time, however, Doris was living in Portland which meant I could leave matters in her hands. She would have to interview members of Daddy's jury and revisit Judge Tooze and Judge Hawkins.

Before leaving for London in February 1954, I visited Judge Hawkins who had presided at my trial, and I visited Oregon Supreme Court Justice, Walter L. Tooze (formerly Judge of the Circuit Court, Multnomah County), who had presided at Daddy's trial. Both judges were sympathetic, saying we had ample grounds for reopening Wes Bowden's case.

Judge Tooze suggested contacting members of the jury at my father's trial, but I couldn't do that because of the pending trip to England. Since I expected to be gone for several months, everything was turned over to Doris, who subsequently visited eight of the twelve members of my father's jury. She also spoke to Frank Hokenyos, who told her he believed Daddy had been unfairly convicted. We were now trying to ensure Daddy's parole. Doris worked very hard during the spring and summer of 1954 to achieve that end.

In fact, she did so well that Mr. John H. Hall (the lawyer retained to oversee our new attempts to reopen the 1946 case, replacing J. Robert Patterson), was able to write to ex-Warden George Alexander, who was in office at the state prison when Daddy first arrived there.

> April 1, 1954
>
> Dear George,
>
> I represent the family of James Westley Bowden who in 1946 was sentenced to life imprisonment for the murder of his wife, resulting from an explosive device contained in a foot locker.
>
> Mr. Bowden was received at the prison in 1946 and is now eligible for parole. I have been retained by the family for that purpose. I have supplied the board with letters from Mr. Bowden's two married daughters, one sister, three brothers and three nieces all living in Portland, who have offered a home and employment. I have also secured a very fine letter from Justice Walter Tooze [see below] who presided at the trial.
>
> "Dutch" Herder [Captain of the guard at the prison during the first four years of my father's tenure], has given me a letter stating that Mr. Bowden's conduct in prison has been beyond reproach. I also have a letter from "Spec" Keene urging that a parole be granted.
>
> I have also been able to trace nine of the original jury which convicted Bowden and they have all signed a letter urging parole. The district attorney of [Multnomah] county has told me that he will offer no objection.

> You were warden of the prison during most of the time Bowden has been confined and of course you know of his record there.
>
> It occurs to me that a favorable word from you will carry great weight with the members of the parole board. If you would drop me a short note recommending that parole be granted or that in your opinion he would be a good parole risk, I know his family will be grateful and I will consider it a personal favor to me [J.H.Hall].

Judge Tooze had written a letter, dated 18 January, 1954, to the State Board of Parole/Probation:

> I am advised that Mr. Bowden is applying for parole and probation. If my memory serves me correctly, he has now been confined in the state penitentiary about seven years.
>
> I sat as the Circuit Judge before whom his case was tried to a jury, resulting in a verdict of conviction. The sentence I imposed upon him was a mandatory one.
>
> There were many extenuating circumstances in his case. At the time of his trial, I entertained a true feeling of sympathy for him. He had at all times before this unfortunate trouble arose been an honest, hard-working, law-abiding citizen, with many staunch friends among people of standing, some of whom testified in his behalf. He had loyally served his country as a soldier. Also, he had been a good husband and father. Had it been within my power so to do, I think, under all the circumstances of the case, and the testimony which I heard, I would have paroled him from the bench.
>
> I think the punishment he has received up to date amply repays his debt to society, and assuming, as I do, that his record as a prisoner has been above reproach and in keeping with his character, I do not

> hesitate to recommend, even urge, that his application for parole be granted. I am sure that society will never again have occasion to deal with him in the criminal courts.
>
> I make this recommendation, believing it to be proper, inasmuch as I was the trial judge.
>
> Respectfully yours, Walter L. Tooze

The full impact of the Parole Board's hearing in November, 1953 wasn't clear until the Judge's letter was answered.[1] I received this short note from Judge Tooze dated January 26, 1954:

> Dear Mrs. Ross: I enclose the letter I just received from the Parole Board. It speaks for itself. I am sorry that the board did not feel justified in granting parole at this time. Perhaps, at the end of the two year period, things will be different. For your sake, and that of your father, I sincerely hope so. I do not know of anything further I can do to help you. I said all that I could say in the letter I wrote them. They now know how I feel about it, and my letter will be a part of his permanent file, and available when next the Board considers the case.

The "enclosed letter" to which the Judge refers was written by H.M. Randall, Director of Parole and Probation and dated January 25, 1954. This letter was puzzling because it was the first time Doris and I had heard anything about psychiatric evaluation:

---

[1] My trial with the Hearst newspapers occurred in October 1953. It attracted enough attention to cause a Parole Board hearing in November the same year.

Acknowledgment is made of your letter of January 18, 1954, regarding James W. Bowden, OSP 18688.

I can certainly appreciate your interest in Bowden, as he apparently is a man who had many friends over the State of Oregon. You possibly also know that he was personally acquainted with Roy S. "Spec" Keene, a former member of this board.

Bowden has finished serving his statutory seven-year minimum, and appeared before our board on November 23, 1953. *A psychiatric evaluation of this man was to the effect he is paranoid and incapable of adjusting in society. There is no definite psychosis present, so that his transfer to the State Hospital is not indicated at the present time; but, it seems to be the feeling of our psychiatrist that psychosis might develop in the future* (italics added).

So that the board might be fully advised and keep close contact with this case, further consideration was continued for two years, with further psychiatric evaluation. I, of course, cannot forecast what action our board will take two years hence, as it will depend considerably on the outcome of the studies which will be conducted during that period; however, I can assure you of our board's interest in Mr. Bowden, and I am certain that interest will continue.

> Very truly yours, H.M. Randall

Something was wrong somewhere. Examining these letters now, I find the dates and times they include highly suspect. Randall's comments to Judge Tooze don't coincide with those the parole board specified to our attorney, Mr. Hall, who was assured that a parole hearing would be held in the late summer or early fall of 1954. This contradicted Randall's statements about "two years" in his letter to the judge. Therefore, on September 10, 1954, Hall wrote:

> *On April 26, 1954, I appeared before the board on behalf of Wesley Bowden* (italics added). At the conclusion of the hearing I was advised that my client's petition for parole would again be considered in the late summer or early fall [of 1954].
>
> *Early in June this was confirmed in a conversation with board member Bud Mallett* (all italics added). At that time he told me Mr. Bowden would have a psychiatric examination in August and that the board would consider the matter in September. I am advised, and the record will so show, that this was confirmed by board action about June 26, 1954.
>
> Mr. Bowden was transferred to the state hospital several weeks ago as an active tubercular. Recently his daughter [Doris, who was, by this time, living in Portland] received a letter from Warden Gladden stating that Mr. Bowden was suffering from tuberculosis and cancer of the lung.
>
> A few days ago inquiry was made of the board as to why Mr. Bowden had not been given a psychiatric examination in August as promised, and the reply received was that Mr. Bowden was "not available" for examination. I do not understand such proceedings. He was just as much "available" in the state hospital as he was in the penitentiary.
>
> I realize that it is the policy of the board not to parole for health reasons alone. But the converse of the rule should also prevail; that a man should not be deprived of a parole for health reasons if he is otherwise qualified. As to Mr. Bowden being a possible menace to society, *the record*

> *will disclose that he has been confined to his bed since April of this year* (italics added), and will in all probability spend the remainder of his life in bed or in a wheelchair.
>
> This letter is in protest to the action of the board in refusing to consider his parole this month after I was notified that he would be considered. The board is aware that I am his attorney and interested in his welfare. Common courtesy would indicate that I should have been notified of any change in plans [Signed: John H. Hall].

The Board reneged on its promise of "continued psychiatric evaluation" in mid-1954, after telling Mr. Hall that Daddy would have another parole hearing in September 1954, based on evaluations that should have taken place in August. Hall's protest evoked another letter from H.M. Randall, September 14, 1954:

> This will acknowledge receipt of your letter of September 10, 1954, directed to Harry V. Collins of our board. Mr. Collins is confined to his home, ill, at the present time, but your letter was brought to the attention of the other Board members at our meeting yesterday.
>
> Our psychiatrist had attempted to see Mr. Bowden while he was still at the penitentiary hospital, but the doctors there felt that such an interview was not proper [One wonders *why* it "wasn't proper"?] and we were, therefore, unable to obtain a psychiatric examination as we had earlier hoped to do. I do not know whether the doctors at the State Hospital will have any objection to Dr. Haugen interviewing Bowden at that institution, and if they do not have such an objection, a psychiatric examination will be conducted in the near future [Signed: H.M. Randall].

In the meantime, many of my father's former friends were not only encouraged, but willing, to write to the parole board on my father's behalf, but the whole thing fell into a well of silence. The group of friends included the then Governor of the state of Oregon, Paul Patterson, who wrote to my father directly:

```
Dear Wes,

I was awfully sorry to hear of your illness
and transfer to the state Hospital. I hope
you will get over this rap. If it is any
benefit to you, I learned of this only
because I made inquiry about your status. I
never believed that the Wes I knew belonged
at 2605 State Street.
                Sincerely yours, Paul Patterson
                [Governor], September 9, 1954
```

We knew that the two deputy district attorneys who conducted the prosecution of my father's case, John Collier and Dan Dibble, had no objection to my father's parole. Collier died in 1952, but on April 23, 1954, Dibble said he had no objection, with the proviso that any written communication regarding the matter would be signed by his superior.

Frank Hockenyos, the man whom Daddy had wanted to kill, but didn't, told Doris he would appear before the Parole board on my father's behalf. Mr. Hockenyos was a key figure in our attempts to get Daddy out of prison because he was the only person who might have something to fear if Daddy were released. However, he believed nothing would happen to himself — or to his sister with whom he lived. At my Dad's trial he heard the same thing everyone did — the reason why Daddy put the bomb in the basement of our house instead of leaving it on Frank's doorstep as he had originally intended was that he was afraid that Frank's sister might get hold of it.

No one, including our new attorney, Mr. Hall, could figure out why the Parole Board was dragging its feet. Why didn't the times coincide? All we knew was that it had something to do with Daddy's refusal to accept medication at the prison's infirmary. We also knew it was somehow associated with a couple of long terms of solitary confinement he'd undergone, but at the time, none of us made the relevant connections.

It was in these crucial days of 1954 while I was in England that so much hung in the balance for my father, but I was in England and neither my sister nor I knew anything about the fact that Mr. Patterson had been disbarred from practice in 1949. As far as we know, no one connected with us was aware that Patterson had been disbarred. Perhaps the parole board dragged its feet on the case because they knew that my father had been wrongly incarcerated and they were afraid of what might happen if he were released, but that is speculation based purely on hindsight. What happened after Daddy received the letter from Governor Patterson is the real story as it unfolded in 1954.

Doris and Uncle Stan decided to try to meet with the Governor. They were given an appointment on Friday, September twenty-fourth, 1954. The interview was more than positive; it fulfilled their most extravagant dreams! The Governor knew us as children, remembering our parents from the old days in Baker, where he and Wes were in the American Legion. He had known Daddy for years. Toward the end of the interview, while Doris and Uncle Stan were present, the Governor dictated a letter granting full pardon to James W. Bowden, but we still don't know if that letter ever got off the secretary's dictation pad.

Governor Patterson said the letter would be delivered to the appropriate people in due course and that the family should make immediate arrangements for an ambulance to take Wes away from the hospital Monday morning, September twenty-seventh, saying he would authorize the move by telephone.

Upon leaving the Governor's office, Doris and Stan visited Daddy in the hospital, where they told him of the assurances they'd received about the Governor's pardon.

They told him that first thing Monday morning he would leave the hospital in Salem and go to my sister's home in Portland.

Wes Bowden died in the prisoner's wing of the Oregon State Hospital sometime after midnight Sunday morning, September twenty-sixth, 1954.

Chapter 8

> So may the outward shows be least themselves:
> The world is still deceived with ornament.
> In law, what plea so tainted and corrupt
> But, being season'd with a gracious voice,
> Obscures the show of evil? ...
> There is no vice so simple but assumes
> Some mark of virtue on his outward parts.
>
> [*The Merchant of Venice*, III, ii: 73]

My sister survived the heartache, sense of loss and torment that, for her, were the results of our father's death. She arranged for his funeral, seeing to his burial in Mt. Calvary Cemetery in Portland on September 30 1954. Auntie Margaret was buried there near him in January 1966, following her own violent death at the hand of her second husband.

Although I grieved for my dad for several years — especially for the misery he endured the last two and a half years of his life — I was spared intimacy with the actual circumstances surrounding his death for a long time.

Doris sent news to me in England that he died, but knowing that Governor Patterson was prepared to issue a full pardon greatly affected my attitude. I believed Daddy was vindicated because of the juxtaposition of death and pardon. I was convinced that for him, dying was a real victory. I remain persuaded about this even today. Somehow, he had to stay alive until some major change occurred in his situation. I think he lost the greater part of his will to live when he was denied parole in November 1953, but he *couldn't* die until the false burden of intention regarding my mother was finally removed. Governor Patterson's promise of pardon did that.

At the same time, I was (and still am) convinced that his death was assisted by transgressions on the part of parole board members and prison authorities. I am even more convinced of this now, having learned (as I did forty-eight years later) that his defense attorney, was disbarred from practice three years after the trial in 1946. One of five "improprieties" for which Patterson was disbarred was the fact that he should never have participated in my father's case under any circumstances (see p. 52).

Apart from that, why else was my father — a man with an exemplary record of prison-behavior — put into solitary confinement, not just for a few days or weeks, but for several months, as he was the last time? Why else was he labeled 'paranoid' when there was no psychosis present and never had been?

Why was it "improper" for the board's psychiatrist to see him, *unless there was something improper for the psychiatrist to see,* given that he was in solitary confinement? Why was the serious terminal nature of his double illness (tuberculosis and cancer) not revealed to my sister until twenty-five days before he died, in spite of the fact that he was transferred to the State Hospital four months *before* she was told about his condition?

H.M. Randall's excuses for the parole board's refusal to release Wes Bowden on parole were indeed "season'd with a gracious voice" — a voice that obscured the fact that, according to information my father gave to his brother, Stanley, he had been told to keep his mouth shut about construction materials that were ordered for a new cell block — materials which never arrived for which he was made to sign *as if they had arrived*. Daddy told Uncle Stan that he was meant to suppress his knowledge that money was pocketed by prison officials that had been earmarked to pay for the materials. That's why he was put in solitary — at least this is the reason my father gave for his punishment. Neither my uncle, my sister or I ever knew the prison officials' side of the story.

In my opinion, it is also why my dad became an angry man towards the end of his life, and why he refused to accept medication from the prison infirmary. Even after his experiences with solitary confinement, he was never angry *because* he was in prison. He became angry because of what he thought he saw took place there.

Neither my sister nor I will ever know if Daddy knew about Robert Patterson's disbarment. As my sister later put it in 1965,

... he understood that it looked to society that he might have done [the murder]. He felt responsible in that he could have prevented it even though he didn't deliberately or intentionally take a life. He worked at the prison and did his best to help rehabilitate every man he came in contact with. He wrote me every week with the same advice and counsel he would have given had I been able to be with him. He did all he could to give us a father we could still turn to, trust and love.

Doris was no stranger to the aftermath of death, but she suffered an increased sense of profound loss because my father's body arrived at the funeral home in Portland already embalmed. The embalming had to have taken place during the twenty-four hours between the time he died and the arrival of his body at a Portland funeral home twenty-four hours later. Embalming, of course, makes autopsy futile.

Doris had enough doubts about the treatment Daddy received during the last two years of his life to want to have an autopsy performed. She needed reassurance that he died a natural death. It wasn't customary for the State to undertake embalming prisoners who died within their jurisdiction. Why was my father a special case?

My sister couldn't get satisfactory answers from anyone: she couldn't discover *why* the embalming had been done. She felt then, and still does, that the sympathetic voices of State Hospital doctors and nurses, the Warden and other prison officials masked the presence of evils that she felt and had premonitions about, but was unable to pin down.

I'm still sorry that I was thousands of miles away when my father died, because I would (literally) have raised hell over the embalming. That's why I wasn't told. I returned from London after Christmas, 1954, and didn't know until 1994 that his body was embalmed before it arrived in Portland.

By the time I arrived home, I could understand how thick were the defensive scars that had formed over my sister's and other family members' psychological wounds. No one wanted to talk about what might have happened to Daddy or how they felt. They didn't want to discuss what had happened to him or to themselves. In particular, no one wanted to talk to me about his death. They were justifiably afraid of how I'd react: I wouldn't have been able to leave well enough alone. I wouldn't have understood why his body was embalmed and I still don't. Nor, as the years pass, do I understand why the promised letter of pardon never arrived from the Governor's office. After finding evidence that my father's attorney, Patterson, acted improperly, I have yet another question to add to the lengthy list of things I don't understand.

In 1954, however, there was the inescapable 'bottom line' about his death that everyone understood: the finality of it all. By dying, Daddy effectively escaped from prison and parole board control. When he was thus released, deliverance of those closely connected to him became possible. For family members, there had been a surfeit of pain. This was especially true, I think, of my sister:

> My father knew he was innocent of the crime for which he was convicted, but he believed in our country and our system and refused to let the family spend any more money on trials or any more attendance in courts and questioning of his teen-age daughters. ... The hardest parts were trying to make people understand that he held no malice or hatred for those responsible [for his being in prison]. It was heartbreaking to have the jurors tell their stories of conscience over eight years. One lady who felt strongly [Daddy] wasn't guilty and held out for a "not guilty" verdict *finally* gave in because it was the week of Christmas and she had children of her own and relatives coming from out of town. For eight years [this woman told me] Christmas had been torture to her.

It is difficult to convey how Doris and I felt about the jurors who finally consented to a "guilty" verdict because they wanted to be home with family and friends for Christmas. Mr. Patterson (the defense lawyer in 1946), had consented to having the trial near Christmas because he thought such timing would be advantageous. I've thought maybe it was the influence of that special time that kept the jury from recommending the death sentence, but Patterson reckoned without humanity's concerns for the local and trivial. In this case, two or three jurors' selfish desires triumphed over thoughts of the consequences their decision would have in our lives. Doris told me about the interviews she'd conducted with eight or nine jurors during my absence, which, for half of them amounted to tales of remorse mixed with relief because of the opportunity of speaking with her. They were haunted by what they had done and asked her forgiveness.

Regardless of how she felt, however, Doris couldn't see herself using the materials she'd collected or pursuing matters further at that time. Apart from anything else, it was a matter of simple survival: she had problems of her own that had to be dealt with. Her five-years-long marriage to Cliff Gentry was in the process of breaking up. She had to get on with her life: there was the house they'd bought in Portland and all the details of a shared life which now had to be separated.

In view of prevailing circumstances, it was impossible for me to blame Doris or try changing her mind; she'd been through enough. We all had. I had to accept the fact that I alone couldn't continue attempts to exonerate his name.

Suddenly, I had no overriding purpose for staying in Portland, continuing on as a dance teacher as I had before going to England while Dorian finished at Portland State College. He had about eighteen months of course work to finish before getting his bachelor's degree and already I could feel the walls of the different picture he now had of what he wanted out of life closing in around me. He wanted a "normal life": respectability and a family.

I was twenty-seven years old in October 1955. By the time my birthday arrived, it became clear that I would never be able to do much more than live in Dorian's shadow. He had obviously grown a great deal while I'd been away, and that was wonderful, but so had I grown.

For the first time, between the ages of twenty-five and twenty-six, I'd been completely on my own: I'd traveled across the northern United States and Canada by myself. I had embarked for England on a ship from Wolff's Pier, Quebec and taken a boat train to London, managing nicely on my own.

For many months, I'd been among people who knew nothing of my background or my father's and mother's difficulties. With an unaccustomed sense of freedom, I threw myself into learning everything I could about teaching and dancing at Sadlers' Wells School along with my students. Actually, I saw very little of them, except in occasional classes, and after two or three months, I spent more time at Audrey de Vos's studio than I did at the Wells.

Gradually, I participated in fewer and fewer classes per week at the Wells, because I found I knew what was being taught there. What I was interested in was *how* dancing was taught in England, especially by de Vos, an extraordinary woman, who, among other things, taught the *prima ballerina*, Beryl Grey. Ms. de Vos was an arch-enemy of Sadlers' Wells School and everything it stood for.

As she put it, "I'm sick and tired of being a hospital for Sadler's Wells dancers." Her complaint was amply confirmed by several of those who studied with her, including Beryl Grey, who told me the tale of injuries sustained at the Wells and her subsequent rehabilitation through de Vos's teaching. Beryl's height was a major problem (she stood five feet ten inches tall in her bare feet and was over six feet tall *en pointe*). Although her height was a technical problem in many ways, it was an asset on stage: her portrayal of the Black Queen's role in de Valois' ballet, *Checkmate*, was spectacular, not only because of her striking physical presence and technical virtuosity, but because of her artistry. She required individualized teaching and was fortunate enough to have found it with de Vos, who first saved, then perpetuated, her career.

The tensions that existed at that time between "the big three" in England's ballet world; Audrey de Vos, Ninette de Valois and Marie Rambert,[1] was instructive. I didn't do classes with Rambert, but attended enough lectures, etc. to understand what she was on about. Much of what she said about the teaching of dancing remained with me for years:

---

[1] Ninette de Valois was responsible for putting English ballet "on the map" so to speak. She was the director of the *Sadler's Wells Ballet* which became *The Royal Ballet*, having established a school in 1926 with Lilian Baylis. Marie Rambert taught many famous dancers and choreographers, among them, Frederick Ashton. She established a school in 1920, and was the founder of *Ballet Rambert*, the oldest English ballet company still performing. Audrey de Vos was a teacher only.

"Artistry begins with the first position" she announced, striding into the classroom, stripping off elbow length gloves that matched her elegant streetwear, at the beginning of a lecture-demonstration with five of her pupils.

"You *must* look at it that way if you teach scrubs — and make no mistake about it — *I teach scrubs*, meaning those who didn't make it into Sadler's Wells School." Her students, of course, not only didn't look like "scrubs," they performed brilliantly, as she pointed out the problems they'd had and how these were overcome throughout long periods of study.

"But," she continued, "it doesn't take much real knowledge to teach dancing at the Wells. Who *can't* teach students with perfect bodies — bodies that have no problems to overcome? I've never had the luxury!"

Ninette de Valois no longer taught technique classes at the Wells — nor had she done for many years — but I remember a demonstration class she gave just after I arrived in 1954 that was equally inspiring (to me, at any rate) as her choreographies.

"Everyone who comes here strives to be a genius" she said, "whether they are potential dancers, choreographers or teachers. What they don't know is that genius in any field breaks rules. But, in order to break rules, you have to know them, and that's where one starts at Sadler's Wells — learning the rules. People who don't know rules *can't* break them. They waste a lot of time pretending."

Years later, when I studied aesthetics with Eugene Kaelin as part of the philosophy courses I took at the University of Wisconsin, I recalled these women's words and the context in which they lived and worked, which was so unlike the American experience. However they may or may not have interacted with one another, these women functioned (as many dance teachers did in Europe) within a centuries-long tradition of an aesthetic institution supported by monarchies. In France and Russia, where the monarchies were overthrown, the institutions were still supported by the State.

Even the British Commonwealth countries shared in the tradition of state-supported performing arts, an advantage that has never been enjoyed, until fairly recently, by American performing artists. Dancers especially, never enjoyed this privilege, unless, of course, one counts the dancers who, like Martha Graham, depended upon support from one of many representatives of America's "economic aristocracy" (the Rothchilds) for her school, her company and the time to choreograph.

The economic plight of the majority of American dancers and teachers functioning in a democracy is very different. Someday, perhaps the history of the performing arts in America will studied — and written about — from this point of view. It would be an illuminating exercise, because many problems faced by American dancers over the years aren't the result of *personal* characteristics. They are the results of political pressures controlled by the social system in which they live and work. However, I didn't think of any of that kind of thing in 1954 while I was in England. I was too busy attempting to absorb as much as I could of the riches that were available. I was able to attend dance performances and the theatre at least three times a week because seats were unbelievably cheap. I went to art museums and walked for miles, enjoying the sense of actually living in the history books I'd read all my life. I discovered I did reasonably well on my own. For the first time in the quarter of a century I'd so far lived, I alone chose what I would do, when I would do it, where I would go and what I would see.

But there was what I imagine would be called these days a "downside" to it. I became aware that the outward shows people put on (including my own) while presenting themselves to others, were generally composed of that which was *least* themselves. Everyday life often hid, rather than revealed, individual realities.

It's hard for others to comprehend the fact that the incident between my parents dominated Doris's and my separate lives for at least eight years. I still can't evaluate how typical my reactions were at the time, but the truth is that I led two distinctly different lives and was careful to keep them apart. The feelings I had for the men I'd married (Olly, for one year and Dorian for seven); for the friends I made and the students I taught were totally unlike those I had about anyone connected with either side of the family.

I'm certain that until I came back from England, where I was by myself among people who knew nothing of my past, I didn't fully understand that *it was possible to free myself from it all*. Up to the time I returned from England, I carried the whole family incident as 'extra baggage'.

It was thus that my inner world became even more divided after my first trip to England. "Knowing where you're at" so to speak, became as important to me as "knowing where you're from."

In spite of the experiences I'd had with my family, I came back from England knowing without any doubt that "The world is still deceived with ornament." I, too, was blind, although I didn't think of it then as deception. I not only rejected *where* I was from, I didn't care much for *what* I was back then, although I never denied any of it to myself or anyone who was interested.

After Daddy died and after living in England on my own, I began focusing more on "where I was at." I could see that where I was in Portland in 1955 wasn't a particularly desirable place to be, so I left the Pacific Northwest in May 1956. I went to New York, where I supported myself by working for painters and sculptors as a model, privately and in schools. I left Portland assuming that I preceded Dorian perhaps by a year. He was supposed to graduate in June 1957 (earlier, if he could manage it), then he would come to New York to join me. We'd always planned eventually to live there.

Besides modeling in New York, I taught ballet classes for Bob Joffrey, who was from the Pacific northwest (he was born in Yakima, Washington). He found my approach to teaching dancing interesting, since (thanks to my students' successes) my reputation as a teacher had preceded me to New York City. Joffrey's studio was located on Sixth Avenue in Greenwich Village, and it was a pleasure teaching for him, although our association didn't last all that long.

I found a vacant loft in September 1956, at 17 West 24th Street (an address in New York's garment district, near the old Flatiron Building). The neighborhood was good for dance studios as the street died at 5:30 p.m., thus no one was bothered by music, drums, etc. playing late into the night. I started my own classes soon after I moved into the place.

New York was (and always has been) good to me (and good *for* me, I think), remembering that I went there the first time during the paradisical end of the 'fifties, when there were still cops on the beat; when the so-called 'drug culture' hadn't ruined the lower Eastside; when there were no *graffiti* on subway trains and when Miles Davis, Charles Mingus, Stan Kenton and others of similar calibre were creating the popular music.

I was especially interested in the studio location I'd chosen for two reasons: it was in the same building on the floor beneath Pearl Primus's and Percival Borde's studio, where I studied Afro-Caribbean dancing, and, it was part of the history of the New York modern dance scene. It had been the location of the old New Dance Theatre before that establishment moved uptown.

After New Dance Theatre moved out, the loft had been a lace factory for a few years. Making the loft into a dance studio again meant sanding and polishing the 72 x 42 foot floor, then treating it with kerosene until the required satin-smooth finish was achieved. It also meant erecting ballet barres down the length of the far-side, and furnishing one end of the room and an alcove so I could live there.

When I look back on this arrangement (which cost the grand sum of $115.00 per month) it is with the greatest of pleasure. I learned so much in New York and I had many adventures. I had a wonderful time in the City during those years, not all of which I spent living in the studio.[2]

When I first moved into the loft at 17 West 24th Street, however, it hardly mattered where I lived, because I taught classes in Long Island and at Silvermine, near Darien, Connecticut, in addition to those I taught in the studio. I studied regularly with Pearl Primus and Percival Borde and, in general, kept myself busy making ends meet. During this time, I felt the need to seek out a doctor.

If I remember correctly, it was because I felt a bit tired occasionally and thought I needed liver shots or a tonic of some kind. I asked my friend, Joffrey, to recommend someone, and as a result,

---

2 Jumping in time for a moment; in 1959, I moved into an apartment on East Fourteenth Street because classes had increased and I had plans for forming a small touring company. There simply wasn't room in the studio for everything.

found myself in mid-October, at (believe this or not!) 10 Downing Street in Greenwich Village not far from the Joffrey studio.

The name on the door read, 'Dr. Harold S. Wadro, MD.' I hadn't had a medical examination for some time, so went through the whole routine. At the end of it, the Doctor said, "Miss Williams, would you like to talk to someone; talk about things that have happened in your life, say, every week for an hour? I am about to qualify as a psychiatrist, and can take some patients. It seems to me you might benefit from these kinds of sessions, because there's nothing wrong with you physically that I can see. You are in spendid health. Unless something turns up in the blood and other samples I've taken, there isn't anything wrong with you."

To this day, I've no idea what prompted him to ask me such a question, but I heard myself responding, "Yes, I'd like that very much. When will we start?"

"How about the day after tomorrow?" he asked, adding, "By that time, I'll have the results of the samples."

"O.K., what time? I can come anytime before five-thirty."

The first appointment was arranged at four p.m. on Thursday; a time that remained pretty much the same for my visits to his office over the next four years (October 1956 to December 1960). I left 10 Downing Street feeling pleased — and, I remember, *curious*. I had no idea how the sessions would go — only that he was right — I *did* want to talk to someone about my life.

The first session amounted to little else than my telling him the tale of my parents' misadventures. I spoke all in a rush. Once started, the words fairly tumbled over one another and fifty minutes seemed a very short time indeed. Dr. Wadro triggered the verbal flood by asking what I believed to be the most important thing that had happened to me in my life, then he said nothing. He just listened, filling his pipe occasionally and nodding now and again giving me his full attention.

When the appointed time was up, he stopped me in mid-sentence by raising one hand slightly off the desk, saying, "There is plenty of time. We'll continue next week. In the meantime, I want to start you on a series of shots which you will take for six weeks; the first today. They're hormone shots and they will make you feel better."[3]

The shots made me feel much better; the tiredness went away, but I soon grasped the fact that when the shots stopped, I could slowly regain the good feelings I had because of them through the talk-sessions. Together, we would work out the emotional problems that made me feel 'tired' as I put it when I first came to him. Nothing had turned up in the blood samples he'd sent to a laboratory for analysis, so we decided that ego-supportive therapy (as he called it) would resolve at least some of my problems. Talking to Dr. Wadro was one of the best things I ever did, and I was soon to realize how lucky I was to start the emotional healing process when I did. Needless to say, perhaps, 1956 was a momentous year for me!

We were to take three weeks off from the therapy during Christmas and the New Year. I planned to visit Grammy in Baker. Since Grandpa died in 1950, she was especially glad to see Doris or me (or both) over the holidays. Doris wasn't able to visit that year, so she was glad that I could manage to get to the west coast. I left for Baker late the twenty-first of December. As I expected Dorian to join me at Grammy's house, I wasn't worried when I couldn't reach him by telephone before I left New York City. I traveled west having no idea that I would end up in Portland, nor did I foresee what would happen while I was there.

Shortly after arriving in Baker, I had a 'phone call from Dorian, from Portland General Hospital, which explained why he hadn't answered my telephone calls to him at our house. He asked me to come to Portland because he wanted very much to see me, but he expected to be in hospital another ten days at least, and would be unable to travel for some time after that. He wanted me to come as soon as possible because we had a lot to talk about which he couldn't discuss over the telephone. Naturally, I said I would come to Portland immediately. I was worried when he told me he had some kind of staphylococcus infection and was in an isolation ward.

---

[3] I don't know why he recommended this particular treatment, nor did I question it. I trusted him implicitly, and, as things turned out, it's a good thing I did.

I left Baker for Portland the day after Christmas. Upon arrival, I telephoned Dorian who had arranged for friends to give me his car and a set of keys to the house. He said I could visit him in the hospital at nine a.m. the following morning.

When I turned up at the appointed time, I thought the nurse's reaction to my presence was odd, but I was so preoccupied with the prospect of seeing Dorian, finding out about his illness and such after my absence since May that year, I paid scant attention. When I told the nurse whom I wanted to see, she asked who I was.

"Mrs. Ross," I said.

She replied quizzically, "Really?"

"Yes. I'm Mrs. Dorian Ross" — adding, "from New York City." Her expression changed from confusion to embarrassment, then she said, "I'm sorry. Let me get you a gown and face-mask."

She explained the rules of the isolation ward to me: I could hug, but not kiss, Dorian; I could hold his hands, but couldn't use any of the dishes or facilities connected with the room. If I wanted water or coffee, for example, I had to ask the nurse. I had to wash my hands with special soap upon entering or leaving the room. When the nurse finished, she conducted me into the glass-enclosed room and disappeared.

My husband looked very handsome lying there, his tousled dark hair against a white pillow, the dark-brown eyes closed, his face turned towards a window touched by the clear morning light. I longed to kiss him, but that was impossible because of the mask covering my face like a middle-eastern yashmak. "It's so *good* to see you" I said several times, lifting his hands and kissing them through the mask. He responded in kind, then we began "catching up" exchanging stories of our lives for the months we'd been separated, even though we'd written to each other at least once a week.

He was telling me how far behind he was with his schoolwork and that he probably wouldn't now be able to graduate in 1957 because of the illness when the door burst open. A red-headed young woman strode into the room, covered up, as I was, by a hospital gown and mask. "I'm Nona" she announced in a harsh, strangled voice, "I'm here to say you have no right to be here. Just *leave* now." She grated the words out.

"Go back to New York where you came from, since you don't want to be Dorian's wife anymore. He's mine now. Just go away and leave us alone." She kept talking, but I didn't hear a word she said, because I was staring at Dorian, trying to absorb the shock. The old familiar double consciousness kicked in.

Dorian looked at Nona, trying to talk to her through the harangue she had going, which, once started, wasn't about to stop. Two or three words penetrated my consciousness: 'baby', 'pregnant' and 'real wife'. Since Dorian clearly had no control over the situation, I darted towards the door calling for the nurse.

"Get her out of here" I ordered tersely when the nurse appeared, "or I won't be responsible for what happens."

The nurse came into the room, looking toward her patient for confirmation. Her presence checked Nona's diatribe, but during the silence that followed, Dorian said irritably, "You *know* you shouldn't have come here. I told you to wait until I called. Please go now. I'll be in touch."

The nurse took Nona's arm, conducting her from the room as she said: "You must leave. I'm sorry, but he's a sick man." Nona protested, saying I should leave too, but she left with the nurse and I never saw her again.

When I was sure she'd gone, I turned toward the bed from the window where I stood during Nona's exit, gazing across the sparkling panorama of Portland, beautiful as always against its background of dark-green foothills and snow-covered mountains. A meliorative silence filled the room until I spoke.

"Who and what" I asked softly, bending slightly towards the sheet-covered figure in the bed, "was *that* apparition?"

"Would you mind telling me just what the hell I'm doing here?"

Chapter 9

> The thing on the blind side of the heart,
> On the wrong side of the
> door,
> The green plant groweth, menacing
> Almighty lovers in the spring,
> There is always a forgotten thing
> And love is not secure.
>
> [*Ballad of the White Horse*, i-iii; bk. iii
> G.K. Chesterton]

Reaching towards me with both hands, Dorian almost whispered, his voice appealing: "Drid, you're the best friend I ever had."

"I can't argue with that" I replied coldly, refusing to touch him. "How long has this been going on? Is she really pregnant?"

"I met her a month or so after you left for New York. For awhile, we were just friends. Then ... well, you know ..." he said lamely, "you've been gone for a long time. I don't know for sure if she's pregnant. Maybe she's just saying that."

"You think I've been gone a long time?" I blurted out, incredulous. " I think not! Seven or eight months isn't long. I've only been gone since May."

I looked at him as if I'd never seen him before. "There are pregnancy tests, aren't there? Or are you so sure I'll stay here now that I know what's been going on that you haven't bothered to find out whether she's really pregnant or not?"

"You still haven't answered my question" I continued, *"what the hell am I doing here?* Why didn't you write about your change of plan and save me the expense of this trip? What if she really *is* pregnant? What am I supposed to do — stay in Portland and look after the three of you — if there is a third?"

"No," he said, looking away from me and down at his hands, "I don't know what I thought. I didn't really *think*, damn it. All I know is I don't want to come back to New York anymore — I know that's what we'd planned, he interjected hastily — but I really want to stay here in Portland. Judd Bierman (his advisor at Portland State College) has a good job lined up for me when I finish school. Nona has always wanted a baby, and she likes being a housewife." The tone of his voice changed. He no longer spoke in low, appealing tones.

"Good for her!" I said sarcastically, "It looks as if she's about to get her wish. You don't expect me to say that what I want right now is to have babies and be a housewife, do you? You know I divorced Olly because he wanted to have babies and that meant I couldn't go to school."

He said nothing — just looked at me pleadingly with soulful brown eyes.

"Let me get this straight," I said. "If I come back to Portland and have a baby, you're willing to dump Nona, even if she's pregnant. And if I go back to New York, you'll marry her and have a family?"

His reply was almost inaudible: "I guess that's about it."

"And what if you find out she's not pregnant and I go back to New York?"

"I guess we'd better get a divorce."

"I won't ask if you're in love with her — or with me, because I think I know what you'd say, and quite frankly, it all seems monumentally irrelevant. I wouldn't believe a word you say anyway — not now, or ever again — so let's get down to brass tacks. What do you want me to do, since I am here, or is this the end of it? Shall I just return the housekeys and the car to Carol and Bill and go back to Baker today?"

"No." he said, glad of an opportunity to change the subject, "There are several things you could do for me if you would."

He outlined a program of seeing his advisor and teachers at Portland State, visiting an old friend, Charles Gaupp, in whose production of Christopher Fry's *Sleep of Prisoners* he was supposed to appear, who needed reassurance that he would be able to perform. He wanted me to contact his creditors in person, make further arrangements for the two Boxer dogs he'd acquired during my absence, etc. As he talked, I made a list.[1]

At the end of the recitation, he said, "I'll make Nona get a pregnancy test. I don't think she's really going to have a baby, and, maybe, after you've seen people and all, you'll change your mind." I felt as if he hadn't heard a word I'd said.

"My God! You lived with me for six or seven years, but you don't know me at all, do you, Dorian?" My bitterness was clearly audible: "There's no way I'd stay here, nor will I ever live with you again, so forget it. Let's just be sophisticated and Noel Coward about the whole thing. I really can't handle anything else." He smiled.

"Good old Drid! That's how I thought you'd react" he said. "You're strong as ever! See you tonight, then, around nine?" He waved to me as I left, but reached for the telephone beside his bed, probably to ring Nona who, for all I knew, was waiting downstairs.

I was numb inside. I was deafened by the noise of slamming doors and very deeply hurt. Later that day I cried, but found myself determined somehow to survive. I clung to the thought of discussing the whole affair with Dr. Wadro. I remained in that state of alternating numbness and pain until I was in his office again in New York two weeks later.

It took the better part of a week in Portland to accomplish the tasks I'd been set because the New Year holiday intervened. I watched peoples' reactions to me like a hawk, wondering if anyone was aware of the changed state of Dorian's and my affairs. Not a single person to whom I spoke, including many old friends, mentioned Dorian's and my relationship, nor did they speak of the future. Nona was never mentioned. It was as if no one knew her or knew what was going on.

---

1 Looking back, I realize I did these things for him at the time because I was 'supposed' to do them, as his wife. I hadn't yet worked my way out of the mechanical, habitual responses to situations that I later discovered governed everything I did.

On the other hand, I was Dorian's wife. I was in Portland doing wifely things for him in his hour of need, and that seemed to be enough. Everyone I met or spoke to appeared glad to see me. They told me how much I'd been missed and one or two of them expressed hope that I would soon return. They apparently enjoyed my descriptions of the New York studio and my life there, and that was that.

In the end, I didn't go back to Baker. I telephoned Grammy to say I would leave for New York from Portland. I couldn't explain to her what had happened between Dorian and me because she wouldn't have understood, mainly because she passionately wanted grandchildren. Because she did, she would surely have encouraged me to stay in Portland. I let her imagine that I was simply upset over Dorian's condition and had to stay longer than I'd anticipated.

The return trip to New York was a nightmare: the plane ride from Portland to Chicago was uneventful, but the second leg of the journey was terrifying because of dreadful weather. We flew through severe storms nearly all the way, and for the first time in my life, I was confronted with a genuine consciousness of physical mortality. I was afraid to die and equally fearful that I would at any moment.

I wasn't the only one who was afraid: my fellow passengers sat tense and apprehensive as the plane dropped a couple of hundred feet then suddenly rose again as it struggled through the air. Not even the pilot's reassurances over the intercom or the stewardesses' ministrations helped drive the fear away. It was a relief to disembark at La Guardia Airport, even though the weather was comparatively tranquil for the last hundred miles of the flight.

As we circled New York City preparing to land, we were treated to a beautiful sunset that outlined the city's lighted skyscrapers with gold. Had the buildings been green, I could have been approaching Oz's Emerald City — the prospect was that serene. Glad to be back on solid earth again, I took a taxi to the safe haven of my studio.

Unlocking the door, I thought, "This is where my life is now. The part with Dorian is over. We'll never share New York. I'm really alone." Then, the tears came in a flood.

Somehow, during the next three days, I taught classes, saw people and all the rest, but I had difficulty coping with the deep feelings of betrayal I felt. There seemed to be nothing I could do about the situation — and *doing* something became all important.

As I returned to the studio from a trip to the grocer's the day before my Thursday appointment with Dr. Wadro, I impulsively walked into an Army Air Force recruiting office. I stayed there over an hour and, before leaving, had filled out and signed an application to join the Women's Air Force. The officers in charge said they would be in touch with me Friday about my application. I felt marginally better: I had taken positive action.

Dr. Wadro wasn't kind when I told him the next day what I'd done. First, he asked me what had happened in Baker.

"Nothing" I said, "except a telephone call from Dorian." Briefly, I outlined the trip to Portland, but was totally unprepared for his response, for I was expecting some sympathy at least.

"Good God!" he exploded, pushing his chair back from the desk with both hands. "Disappointed in love, so you're off to join the Foreign Legion, is that it?"

"Do you have any idea what life in the Air Force is like?" he continued, "I do, because I was in it during the war. Do you have any idea what life in the Air Force would be like for someone like you?"

As I slowly shook my head, considerably shaken by his forceful tone of voice, he answered his own question:

"What you're *really* doing is committing psychological suicide, and that's the truth. What do you want to do that for? I can't stop you, of course, but up to now, I've believed you to be an intelligent woman. Now, I'm not so sure." He busied himself with tobacco pouch and pipe, as he almost, but not quite, turned his back on me.

I burst into tears, but tried to keep my voice steady: "I don't know why I applied for the Air Force, but *damn* Dorian. How could he do this to me? He's lied and cheated and now he's got another woman pregnant." Doggedly, I continued:

"Nona had a test done the day after she came to the hospital and she *is* going to have Dorian's baby — at least he believes it's his baby, and that's enough. He's done everything he promised me he wouldn't ever do, knowing that I divorced Olly because of not wanting to have children just now, but somehow, the baby and Nona aren't the worst of it. He broke our contract! He didn't keep his word."

"Olly and I made an agreement about how our lives would go, then, when push came to shove, he ignored it. Dorian and I made an agreement too. Now he's broken our agreement. I just don't understand how he could do the same things Olly did. Didn't the plans we made mean anything to either of them? Are the years Dorian and I spent together *nothing*?" For awhile, there was silence.

Dr. Wadro spoke gently: "What's important for you is to understand how you feel about it and to work out what you really want to do. Look at me."

I uncovered my wet face from behind my hands. "Can we do that? I feel terrible. I'm hurting. All I can see right now is that my life is in a shambles and I'm completely alone."

"Well, you wouldn't be any less alone in the Women's Air Force, that's for sure. When they call tomorrow, just tell them you've changed your mind. Tell them you're thinking about it and you'll call them back in a couple of weeks."

Through the gnawing pain I felt, I also experienced a curious sense of relief. Over the next few weeks, well into March, we worked through my relationships with the men I'd known: Daddy, my uncles, Mel Grow (the first serious boyfriend), Olly and Dorian.

The dénouement of my marriage to Dorian came a month later, when I received a long letter from him, which Dr. Wadro and I read together. It was a vindictive, rambling letter telling me how I'd dominated his life; how he'd never been happy; how I'd prevented him from doing what he really wanted to do. At one point, Dr. Wadro asked, "Why did you leave him?" I responded instantly, "Why did he let me leave him?"

I still couldn't grasp the fact that I was meant to understand my role in the relationship. I was still looking for others to blame.

Dorian's extended rationalization for leaving me ended by announcing that he'd initiated divorce proceedings in January shortly after I left Portland. His formal complaint against me rested, legally, on desertion, although by the time the actual papers arrived, I couldn't have cared less what reason he thought he had for divorcing me. I was glad to be rid of him and the marriage, because I finally realized that nothing new or different could happen to me until I first emptied everything out of my life from inside.

Like everyone else I knew, I'd worked hard to "fulfill myself" as the saying goes. That is, I looked for fulfillment outside: first in the marriage to Olly, then in the marriage to Dorian. Neither had worked out. Filling myself full of emotion (which is what I basically thought 'fulfillment' meant) obviously didn't work. Chesterton was right: Dorian wasn't a knight on a white horse by any means. I'd been blind to many things in our relationship. Unknowingly, I'd tried to create an image of him, which is precisely what I didn't want him (or anyone) to do to me.

Being able to look at my life from the protected atmosphere of the weekly sessions in Dr. Wadro's office meant that gradually the double consciousness I'd lived with for so long disappeared. After I returned to New York after the New Year had begun in 1957, it slowly transformed into something wholly 'other' as I gradually developed the capacity to see my life from different levels, then to move among these levels at will. *I finally realized that I had choices.*

How can I best explain what I mean by that? Perhaps by spelling out the metaphorical picture I developed of psychological levels, which for me, related to an experience I'd once had in Utah.

Emotionally, I could be buffeted by a storm in a valley, so to speak, or I could climb out of the maelstrom onto a hillside — a real picture of levels — reflecting what I'd experienced while visiting friends who took me on a tour of Salt Lake City.

One of the stops we made that afternoon was to look at the murals in one of the city's public buildings perched high on one of the many hills surrounding the city. It was sunny that day, with a few high clouds in the eastern sky. After enjoying murals, sculpture and architecture for an hour, we emerged into the sunshine where a spectacular view awaited us. A storm complete with thunder and lightning had gathered over the city, but hadn't touched the hills or the building's entry where we stood.

"It's a type of summer storm which often occurs here" my friends told me. "It rains in the city but doesn't reach this high."

I'd never seen a whole storm before, contained, as it were, in the bottom half of the huge bowl in which Salt Lake City is situated. To see the storm from a safe vantage point on the rim of the bowl was remarkably exhilarating.

"It must be pretty awful down there" I observed.

"Oh, it is for a few minutes" my friends agreed. "We've been caught many times. What's interesting is that down there when you're *in* the storm, you can't see the heights where we are."

"No, I don't suppose you can" I replied, "because you'd be too busy dodging lightning bolts and trying to stay dry."

One of the great things about a successful therapeutic process is the new connections it enables one to make and create. The image of hills and valleys regarding internal states was one of the new connections for me. Successful therapy doesn't mean you don't have the equivalent of emotional storms again in your life. What it *does* mean is that you relate to them differently. And, you lose the sense of being at the mercy of everything and everybody. You somehow know that you are in control. Not only does one's inner landscape widen and deepen immeasurably, the landscape has a definite vantage point.

It was from a completely changed viewpoint, then, that I greeted the process server who turned up at my New York studio during the first week in April 1957. He didn't know that he was being addressed from a sun-drenched hilltop in Utah!

He was a nervous little man and, like the rabbits he resembled, he was erratic of manner. Doubtless his profession served to amplify his twitchy characteristics, for he froze into stillness at my every move, appearing terrified that I would do him bodily harm.

He was clearly astonished by my actions: I took the papers he handed over, greeting him warmly with great enthusiasm. Inviting him in for a cup of coffee, I told him I was never so glad to see anyone in my life! He drank the coffee hurriedly, shaking his head in disbelief at the unexpected turn of events.

I tried to persuade him: "Don't worry" I reassured, chuckling, "I'm not crazy. I'm just *happy* because for the first time in my life, I'm free of a whole lot of stuff I don't need." I didn't expect him to understand — all I was interested in was having one person understand my life at that point in time — me. There is a sense in which the key word was 'choice'.

I'd spent most of my life up to mid-1956 and the move to New York dealing with things, people and situations which had *happened to* me. I hadn't *chosen* any of them. Even when I did choose, the choices weren't active. I grew to learn that my choices in the past were largely re-active — a wholly dissimilar matter. None of us choose the families in which we find ourselves, nor do we choose the language we speak or the socio-historical, political and religious circumstances into which we are born. Chosen or not, however, we have to deal with all of it (or not deal with it, as the case may be). Maybe I now indulge in a long-winded way of saying that discovering choice is what growing up is all about; but I believe that having choices and being accountable for them is basic.

I left Portland because my field of choice became too narrow — something I'd learned during the trip to England. Let me add that I don't think moving to another place is something everyone has to do. I've known people who've altered their lives as drastically as I did without relocating their lives three thousand miles away. But for me, the geographical distance was important. As things turned out, moving to New York in 1956 was merely a beginning.

Over the past forty years, I've lived in West Africa for three and a half years, in England for seven, then back to the United States for ten years. Next came five years residence in Australia, then three years in East Africa. Unlike my sister, I'm a nomad. Traveling that much, I know now that however 'new' the surroundings may seem, there's always one familiar person present — one's self. In New York in mid-1957, I hadn't yet learned that.

Back then, awareness centered around the fact that I was twenty-nine years old, I'd established a successful studio in one of the toughest cities in the country and, with Dr. Wadro's assistance, I was working on my life. That life wasn't always a bed of roses by any means but it was fun. It was challenging and it was my own, whatever else it was. And, I was dancing or teaching dancing every day, which I loved.

I was first fascinated by New York City, then I grew fond of it, eventually claiming it as my own (as everyone does). It was a process of accumulating impressions of the City that were peculiarly mine. For instance, I often took a subway train to the docks just before sunrise to watch the fishing boats come in. When you hail from the mountains, the ocean and the many activities surrounding it are new experiences.

The docks are a bustling, noisy scene where, among stacks of 'swordies', halibut and tuna, jostling baskets of clams, shrimp, lobster and crab, spirited haggling went on between hoteliers and fisherman. After watching for some time, I'd have a hot bowl of chowder at Jerry's Clam Bar, then go home — 'home' being my studio, not the house I shared with Dorian in Portland.

I treasured the rides I took on the Staten Island Ferry (still five cents to the Island and five cents back to Manhattan). The Buddhist Monastery and Museum on the top of the island's hill were such a pleasure! I liked the atmosphere there as much as I enjoyed visiting the many leather and sandal shops under the Brooklyn Bridge.

Many late night hours found me on the beach wading in a cold surf, looking out over the ocean under a star-filled sky. All I had to do was turn around quickly to change the scene, for behind me thousands of lights from Coney Island's glittery midway twinkled and flickered over the roller coasters, ferris wheel and merry-go-round — the whole cotton-candy world of a carnival.

I enjoyed walking in Chinatown, window-shopping, eating hot steam cakes when it was snowy and cold or watching people skate in front of Rockefeller Center. I spent hours in the Museums and Sculpture Gardens when it was fine. New York at the end of the 'fifties was a marvelous place!

Nineteen fifty-six and fifty-seven were important years for me: I not only discovered "The thing on the blind side of the heart," as Chesterton put it, but I had hints of an idea that there was something far more important to being human that I was still missing.

"The spirit is the true self." I'd heard such statements all my life, not paying much attention, far less asking, "But what is this 'true' self, if there is such a thing?" Talk about 'self' wasn't real to me, nor was my daily life conducive to finding out much about it (or so I thought). In spite of my recent intimations of mortality (conveniently forgotten almost immediately), I had become smug — even complacent.

It wasn't a state in which I was permitted to stay for very long: the experience I was to have with Walter Chappell the first week in June, 1957 was electrifying, not only because it would mark the second time my life took a right-angled turn, but because I found my Self through the meeting with Walt.

Looking at the written phrase — 'I found my Self' — the words appear ridiculous. Why not, 'I found myself'? Why make an issue of 'self' and 'Self'? The answer to those questions lies in differentiating one's 'Self' out of a field of many 'selves' — the major psychological (some would say, 'spiritual') outcome of my encounter with Chappell.

William D. Smith, an old friend with whom I'd attended ballet school in Portland years ago, invited me to Rochester, New York, for a long weekend visit. He lived with Minor White, whom he wanted me to meet. Bill wanted to renew our friendship. I hadn't seen him since I'd started a studio and a career in New York.

Wes Bowden (1916-17)

Fern, Shirley and Doris (1934)

Fern Chandler
High School Graduation
(1918)

Fern and Shirley
(1930)

Mormon Basin in the late '30s

Drid and Dorian Ross, 1952

Walter Chappell

Drid Williams
(circa 1957-58)

The darkroom door, the stove
and table at Minor's place

Reproduction courtesy the Minor White Archive, Princeton University.

Copyright ©1982 by the Trustees of Princeton University.

All rights reserved.

Mustapha Tettey Addy

He does a Kpanlogo step (K is silent) wearing what is called a Batakari from the North of Ghana.

Addy and his brother, Yacubu

The brothers play Ga drums. Addy (left) is playing Obrenton and Yacubu is playing Prentia.

Chapter 10

> *Not equal to   equivalent to*
> *Not metaphor equivalence*
> *Not standing for .... but direct connection*
>   *to invisible Resonance*
>
> [Minor White, *mirrors, messages, manifestations*, p. 41]

I arrived at 72 North Union Street in Rochester, New York, on the morning of June 6, 1957. Minor White's home was unlike any I'd ever known because of its sparse, Zen-like simplicity, and because it was essentially a place of work. Minor's own photographic work was done there plus many of his students' projects. He created the professional photography magazine, *Aperture*, there. He frequently held short workshops and classes at his upstairs loft-apartment, so there were always people around, discussions going on, meditation in adjoining rooms, and meals being made — all activities punctuated by constant traffic in and out of the basement darkroom. Among the group who were present that weekend was Walter Chappell, who had "arrived on the doorstep of 72 North Union Street shivering in the last snow at the edge of spring."[1] Of his approach to Minor's place, he said, "Upon entering this spacious atmosphere, I sensed the actuality of my footprints standing between the parallels of the known and the unknown."

My entry into Minor's home didn't include that kind of consciousness, nor did I know that the atmosphere there was largely the result of his lengthy studies of Gurdjieff's ideas and the development of Edward Weston's and Alfred Stieglitz's concepts, especially the *Equivalent* tradition.

> The idea of equivalence is an equation that is all at once. It takes in the entire mind. Everything works for a moment. The blessing of the photographic image is the precision involved. There is no

---

1 The Threshold of Vision: Minor White. IN *Minor White. A Living Remembrance. Aperture.* No. 95, Summer, 1984, p. 21.

chance, except the chance that there is an intelligent being who will press the shutter at the moment of the equation. Then the image stays as a cogent emblem of eternity. Photography allows you to do that. It insists that you be there" (Chappell 1984: 23).

Walt's words, "be there" are important because his message to me consisted of the fact that I never really was where I seemed to be at any given moment.

I wasn't aware of any of this at the time, nor was I aware that Chappell had met Minor in 1941. When I arrived in Rochester, Walter was merely one of several people I met. After a curt, somewhat dismissive initial greeting, he ignored me. I didn't notice Walt's abruptness, far less care about it, because I was basking in the fulsome admiration and attention of others who were there. They were interested in me, not only because I danced, but because I was Bill's friend. As for me, I was in a holiday mood, making the possibility of a significant encounter the furthest thing from my mind.

Several of the artists present asked to photograph me when they found out I was a sculptor's model as well as a dancer. These young men, I discovered, were vitally interested in the art of movement generally. They saw movement (especially dancing) both as an art form and as an important means of communication. I was happy to work with them. More accurately, I think, the flags of my conceit were all up and flying. The hard work and inconvenience of modeling was a small price to pay for flattery and attention, thus I posed for Minor and for several students soon after I arrived. Minor's loft-apartment was stripped to the bare essentials and he had a sheltered rooftop space which was admirably suited for such work. The next day, everyone looked forward to going on an excursion to William Gratwick's estate (a favorite place of Minor's near Rochester) for continued working sessions.

After a relatively short mid-day meal, seasoned with lively discussions about "equivalents" and "sequences" with which I was fascinated, plus animated, arcane, exchanges among the photographers regarding film speeds and the Zone System, none of which I understood, Walt asked if I would pose for him. Since I hadn't refused anyone else's request, I consented, having no idea what posing for Chappell would entail.

For a start, he wanted to photograph some dance movements nude, so the two of us retired to the seclusion of the roof-top, where I followed his directions (or so I believed) to the letter. After an hour or so, he thanked me, saying he had what he wanted. Apart from noticing an intense energy that flowed from him which seemed very different in quantity and quality from that which emanated from others, I paid very little attention to him.

Bill was upset by my disappearance onto the roof with Walt. He thought I made a poor showing as a guest since I spent more time with Minor's students than with my host, and of the students, I spent more time with Walt. Later at dinner time I tried to rectify the situation — a dinner which featured broth from Minor's famous "continuous soup-pot" (always simmering on the back of the stove) and his tasty variations on Asian cookery, with which he experimented.

Walt had withdrawn into the nether regions of the darkroom after our session on the roof-top. He didn't participate in the merriment or the spirited talk about art that accompanied the evening meal. Some time afterwards, however, he appeared, asking if I wanted to see the photographs he'd taken, saying they were in the kitchen. And they were — at least a hundred or more of them — some displayed on the large top of a plywood table that served Minor both as work and eating space.

I expected to see the poses I knew Walt had taken on the roof-top and a few portraits of which I was aware that were taken in the living room. I didn't expect to be confronted with scores of photographic images of myself I didn't know he'd taken. Amid comments from Bill, Minor and the others about liking this one or that one, exclamations about interesting technical variations, etc., I looked first at the images, and then at Walt, who observed the whole scene dispassionately — as if from a great distance — waiting to see how I would respond.

His lean, elegant body was propped against a wall across the table. He had a faint smile on his lips. Keen falcon's eyes, glinting now and then with amusement, gazed in my direction through a thin translucent tendril of cigarette smoke. He didn't *say* anything, but he didn't have to. Everything he had to say was there on the table in the composite of images in front of me.

I looked at the bewildering array of photographs again. Here was a woman who looked like a baby about to cry. Here was an Amazon — a tower of vitality and strength. Here was an image of a woman who was soft and cuddly as a kitten, but next to her was someone whose steely gaze rivaled the Medusa. Here was an old woman, face frozen into a mask of grief, but over there was a virgin whose April-innocence contrasted sharply with an image revealing a vapid creature — even dull-witted — which was antithetical to the mean, conniving glance of the character depicted in the image next to her. But, over there was an image that exposed a shrew: coarse, insensitive, demanding. Yet another photograph recalled an image of a Byzantine Madonna.

"They're all me," I thought, "and I don't even know half of them. I recognize them, but don't know who they are. *What — or where — is this person?*" I asked myself, meaning the whole conglomerate taken together. I couldn't answer. Nor could I answer Bill, who at that moment pointed to one of the images and said to me, "This is *awful*. You do *not* look like that."

Addressing Walter, he challenged: "How could you take so many photographs that don't look like Drid? Minor says you are an excellent technician, but you don't see Drid as she is, except, perhaps, in one or two of these." The latter announcement was made accompanying his hand moving in a squashed circle over the table.

Walt didn't reply. It was as if Bill hadn't spoken or wasn't there. Nor did I reply to Bill's querulous comments, although he let me know later he took umbrage because I had nothing to say to him. In fact, I was annoyed because he interrupted my thoughts. Furthermore, I couldn't say anything because Bill obviously believed Walt didn't see me as I was.

Nothing could have been further from the truth. Walt was the only person I'd ever met who *did* see me as I truly was: a mass of 'selves' shifting around inside their framework as pieces in a kaleidoscope randomly jostled from the outside. In any case, Bill's impressions and remarks were irrelevant: I knew there was no one inside who was aware of the whole show, except, perhaps, the Self whose attention was riveted on the images spread over the table.

But, by this time, everyone else had returned to the living room except Bill, Walt and me. Bill urged me to come with him — he wanted to rejoin the others, but I couldn't move. Finally, he left the kitchen alone, disgusted, but there was nothing for it — I *had* to keep looking at those pictures! I had to find out what was going on, for a variation of the split in consciousness had again occurred. Some self watched me look at the images, and when I raised my eyes to look at Walt again, I was staring into the lens of a camera. I hadn't noticed Walt's transition to photographer yet again, but I was there with him.

Time, as we ordinarily conceive it, became meaningless from that instant on. The best I can do describing the experience is to speak metaphorically, although it is with some apology, because I'm not a poet.

Time thickens and condenses; voltage rapidly increases, so that glances, words, touch — all the senses are purified — instantly refined. The perceivable world is transformed: taken to some parallel, invisible dimension where it is suffused with light. It is 'of' light — that is, 'de'-light. Some deep well-spring of infinite joy is uncovered that bubbles and dances its way upward toward the sun, broadening into a fantastic fountain, sparkling and twinkling, to fall shimmering into a wide river rushing toward a distant sea. One is exultant — omnipotent — free. I wanted to run, to dance, sing or shout. Actually, I could neither move nor speak. I looked from the camera's lens into Walt's eyes and knew that he knew what was happening.

The photograph he took of that instant in ordinary time is lost, along with all the images from that period. They were destroyed in the fire that annihilated his house in Wingdale, New York, together with all of his belongings in 1960. There is a sense in which the image itself isn't destroyed however, for I remember it as clearly now as when I first saw it: a four-by-five record of a plain face devoid of expression, except for the eyes, which stare trance-like out of the picture-plane.

This image (the one on the bit of photographic paper) and all the others taken then no longer exist, but the time itself isn't lost. In ordinary reckoning, that stretch of time lasted until late Sunday afternoon, June 9, 1957, when I returned to New York and to my studio, never to be the same again. Its equivalent is in æon — another word for eternity. The spirit, once liberated, simply is. The knowledge of the mysterium; the bliss is what remains throughout the rest of one's journey, whatever it may be.

"And where" you may ask, "is the sphere of 'thick time' — condensed time?" It, too, exists, like the Self, because it partakes of infinity. It isn't bound to the finite games of the so-called real world. Nor was I bound to stand, speechless, as if in a trance, across the table from Walt that night. We talked, moved, joined the others, but something like a laser-beam of light connected us and we moved, simultaneously in two worlds, or, as Walt might put it, we moved "between the parallels of the known and the unknown."

There were those present who noticed and those who didn't. Nothing had changed, yet, for me everything had changed, just as it had in 1946 — only this time, it wasn't simply an emotional flash-freeze as the experience with the detective had been twelve years before, nor did the expansion of my consciousness solidify my lesser selves into something resembling a sculpture garden or a graveyard, as the flash-freeze had done.

On the contrary, I moved light as thistledown borne aloft on a warm summer's breeze; spoke little, but melodiously; saw others surrounded by halos of light; tasted full and subtle flavors, and heard, for the first time, overtones and harmonies in music I didn't dream existed. I understood for the first time what I had played in the last piano concert I gave in Portland. I knew that my father — and my mother — were all right. An equivalent, you see, is a simultaneity. Charles Mills, a composer I worked with in New York once told me that he sometimes heard music this way. Not all, but some, of his compositions came to him all at once — in their entirety. Parts of his magnificent *Crazy Horse Symphony* had been like that.

A list of everything I understood during the ninety-six hours that followed: the memorable incidents that took place, such as meeting two Irish wolfhounds, the beating of starlings' wings against an upstairs window, the workout of Gurdjieffian movements in a wooded dell somewhere on the Gratwick estate, and much else, would be as long as it would be tedious or meaningless to others. Wittgenstein was right: "Whereof one cannot speak, thereon one must remain silent."[2] I refer to these experiences in an essay I wrote for Minor's memorial,[3] and find, now, that I can only refer to them again, having discovered that to many people they seem commonplace — over-dramatized, perhaps — but in the end, nothing unusual.

I imagine Minor had some idea of what was going on between Walt and me during that June weekend. I know we talked at length about these (and other) equivalences during the cross-country trip I made with Minor in 1962 through Utah's *Capitol Reef*, an emblem of which are the photographs in his *Sequence 17*. In Rochester during 1957, Minor wrote:

> To a student asking: To photograph what Else things are? When you try to photograph something for what it is, you have to go out of yourself, out of your way, to understand the object, its facts and essence. When you photograph things for what *Else* they are, the object goes out of its way to understand you. Does that help? (*mirrors, messages, manifestations*, p. 111).

Michael Hoffman remembers Minor and 72 North Union Street in the Preface to the Second Edition of "*mirrors and messages ...*" with what is perhaps the greatest tribute that anyone can give to a teacher: "Minor did not manipulate people or settings for his own ends. Instead, he generated an atmosphere enabling others to discover unexpected capacities of their own."

It didn't matter that 72 North Union was "a ramshackle three-story frame building beside an arterial highway" nor did it matter that "Students slept in the attic, where snow blew in through a broken window." Why didn't these things matter? Enduring work was generated there, simply because external surroundings were of secondary or tertiary importance.

---

2 *Wovon man nicht sprechen kann, darüber muss man schweigen* (*Tractatus Logico-Philosophicus* 1922: 1: 7).

3 Creating the Space. IN *Aperture,* No. 95, pp. 72-74.

Minor's teaching did not marvelously open minds. It calmed, allowing one to shed habitual attitudes and conventional critical standards. He induced a sense of shorelessness and of openness (Hoffman 1982: Preface).

He made it possible to pierce and be pierced by a barb of infinity.

Minor's influence and that of his students, especially Walt Chappell and Paul Caponigro, had profound influences on me. My life would have been very different had I not known them, and there are people like that in everyone's life, just as there are people who seem to make no difference at all. For me, the difference lay in the quality of ideas. Perhaps more important, I saw that I had choices. Now, I was no longer a victim of circumstance, living in a pre-ordained universe. I was an active, controlling participator in my life. None of it would have meant much, however, had it not been for Dr. Wadro, whose patience, guidance and care I enjoyed until the end of 1961, when the therapy ended. I will never forget that day.

All the way to the Doctor's office from the studio, a song ran through my head. "Ding-dong the witch is dead — the wicked witch." I hummed as I got off the subway and walked towards Downing Street. The light was beautiful, as it can be sometimes in New York, pouring late afternoon gold into the streets and onto the buildings. As I entered the office, a thought crossed my mind: "I don't have anything to say," but in my light-hearted mood, it didn't matter.

After filling his pipe, Dr. Wadro looked at me quizzically: "You're in a good mood" he said, "how are you *really*?"

"I feel fine, and I don't really have anything to say."

"Hmm . . . I can't believe *that*" he said, smiling.

"You see, I know who you really are."

"Now that's interesting. And who am I?"

"The Wizard of Oz."

"And who was he?"

"He was a little man who sold patent medicine in Kansas" I replied. "He was a magician, really, who appeared to

Dorothy as a mighty voice, a beautiful woman, a roaring lion and a great king — but these were illusions, although she didn't know it at the time. The wizard set tasks for Dorothy and her friends to do because she wanted to get back to Kansas from Oz, so she did everything he told her — especially killing the wicked Witch of the West. But when she got back to the Emerald City, she found out that the wizard was just a plain ordinary person, like she was." I paused for breath.

"Well now, that's something," he remarked, "not many people ever find out such things. Tell me, how did Dorothy kill the witch of the west?"

"She threw a bucket of water on her, but water is really truth. She killed the witch by telling the truth and seeing the truth, 'cause the witch was really Dorothy's mother (but not really — that's who the witch was to me). It's just that Dorothy got blown into Oz, and after awhile, she wanted to go home to Kansas again — except she also liked Oz very much so she wanted to be able to go back and forth from Kansas to Oz whenever she wanted."

"Was she able to do that?" he asked.

"Yes, 'cause the second time she came back to Oz, she got hold of the Nome King's magic belt — that was when she freed Princess Ozma from a spell that turned her into a boy. Ozma showed her how to use the magic belt to get to Oz anytime she wanted. Oh - the second time she came back to Oz, it was because of Glinda, the good Witch of the South, who was a powerful sorceress. You know they got Glinda all wrong in the movie, don't you?"

"I expect they did" he said. "Hollywood isn't known for getting things right. But you haven't told me what happened to the wizard."

"He tried to go back to Kansas with Dorothy, but that didn't work, because she got back the first time by using the red shoes. He finally went back in a hot air balloon that blew him across the Deadly Desert, but Dorothy met him in Oz again. He ended up staying in Oz forever because he liked being a wizard better than he liked selling patent medicines. He and Dorothy were always good friends. The Tin Woodman, by the way, became king of the Winkies, the Scarecrow ruled the Munchkins and the Cowardly Lion lived in Ozma's palace, but they all had many adventures whenever Dorothy came to visit."

There was a long, silent pause, then he said, "Drid, I don't think you need to come back next week, unless you want to, of course. I think you really do know who I am, but the best part is, you know who you are."

That was the last time I saw Dr. Wadro. He died suddenly of a heart attack early in 1962, which was the year I ruptured my left Achilles tendon. The injury ended the dance company and my career as a professional dancer.

I dismantled the studio and left New York late in September 1962, arriving in Minnesota where I stayed with my sister while the tendon healed.

Chapter 11

> I tell you that your daily bread
> is as certain as the day itself:
> your bread is what the day brings with it.
> You hold your own life in your hands
> as a pledge for your food;
> concern for your life is concern for your bread;
> loaf follows loaf to the edge of the grave.
>
> [Hakim Sanai *The Garden of Reality*, 25]

The ruptured Achilles tendon turned out to be the well-known blessing in disguise. Had the injury not occurred when it did, I'm sure I'd have stayed in New York and continued dancing. I wouldn't have gone to University in Wisconsin in 1963, nor would I have started graduate work in social anthropology at Oxford in 1970. Life would have been very different, and in many ways, much more boring.

"*Boring!*" a friend of mine exclaimed incredulously before I left New York in October 1962. "How could being a performer possibly be boring? Being a dancer is *glamorous*. Don't you miss all the excitement and applause? Aren't you *devastated* at the prospect of never going on stage again? I felt so *sorry* for you when I heard about the injury!"

And maybe that's the problem. My friend wanted to feel sorry, wanted to sympathize. She wanted to emphasize the deprivation she was convinced I felt, and I know I never really persuaded her that her generous feelings were misplaced in my case. She could only see me hobbling around on crutches with a boot cast on my lower left leg, where two months previously, she had attended rehearsals in which (presumably with little or no effort), I literally 'flew' — 'conquered gravity' and all the rest of the metaphors attributed to dancers. To think of me as 'grounded', probably for the rest of my life, was a major catastrophe to her, but not to me.

New York has been good to me: psychologically, I grew up there, thanks to Dr. Wadro and the photographers with whom I remained friends, especially Walt, who understood what it means to be alone; that is, 'all-one'. And, I will never forget the space in which I worked in New York. It is part of me.

I clearly remember the seventy-two by forty-two foot studio in which I survived for two out of the seven years I lived in the City. It had a tiny kitchen, dining room and lounge partitioned off at the alley-end of a building on West Twenty-fourth Street between Fifth and Sixth Avenues. My bedroom was a cubby-hole at the street-end of the loft, next to three huge north windows, reaching almost the full height of the seventeen-foot-high ceiling.

The cubby-hole doubled as a dressing room for students and company members when they turned up for class or rehearsals between six and eleven at night after the street died. Then, drums, tape-recorders and piano didn't disturb anyone. The photographer who occupied the first floor studio had gone home. Pearl Primus and Percival Borde, who had their apartment-*cum*-studio upstairs, made lots of noise at the same time my musicians and drummers did. No conflict descended from above, but the contrast between the night songs and dances of the people who inhabited the place between five-thirty and midnight and the silences in which I worked, sweated and battled alone with the archangels was profound. Silence, space and light were masters in that place: the stillnesses out of which significant gestures and actions were born.

My body was the 'paper': the embodied moves, the 'text'. I was (and still am) both writer and reader; speaker and listener; mover and watcher — and I am both mover and moved. If I am not moved, no one else will be.

The walls of the room were off-white, and so was the ceiling twelve feet above my head. I would raise my eyes, but not to look *at* the ceiling. No. I saw beyond the ceiling into limitless dimensions — 'the back of beyond' so to speak, which one can only really see with closed eyes.

Faint, ever-so faint, the street sounds echoed from the garment district in New York all around this room, throbbing; a reality that hustled and bustled purposefully, although unconsciously and mechanically, through its daily routine, while I? I struggled for the street's opposite. Where was the hub of the wheel I sought; that core of silence out of which everything came and to which it will all return? It is here; here where I stand, suspended in a globe of silence, grateful that at last, I can sense the energy's arrival.

Better now acquiesce to gravity, bow the head, curl the shoulders inwards, bend — bend and give in, become an insignificant bump on the smooth plane of friend-floor. Now the satiny wood against my forehead, backs of hands next to obedient feet and knee bones; the lingering scent of oil that keeps the sanded wood mellow and soft to the touch. Yes, it is from here that this dance will begin; from this yielding, embryonic shape.

From that egg-like shape[1] the dance will grow: first through the arms, because that's where the energy is beginning to gather strongly.

Working with movement isn't like working with words or color, stone or paint, sound or clay. Somebody once said that color, sound, stone *and movement* are natural elements, but I say no to that. Nobody's movement is 'natural', except for a few weeks, maybe, after they're born. The movements of the winds are natural and we don't create them, but the moves we make all the time aren't like the wind, except metaphorically, because human beings have *conceptions of* moving. Like words (but not the same as words), gestures and acts/actions are the creations of people — and of groups of people — and they are above all language-tied.

Let yourself feel the silence, sense the space around you, be aware of the energy flow, savor the light — use these aesthetic apperceptions as guides, constantly making decisions: which part will move now, where will it move and how? How much energy will I release with that jump? How much will I hold back? As it were, listening to the body — being supremely receptive.

[1] It was from that position that *Forms One* began — a major, thirty-minute piece of choreography to a musical score composed by Charles Mills.

If you're Alicia Makarova, you ask Ninette de Valois, "how do I feel when I stab him [The Red King in Checkmate]? Do I know I'm going to kill him or is it an accident?" Or, "Why can't I do a high *developpé* in the dance with the Red Knight?"

If you're Daniel Nagrin, you do a dance with a West African mask called "Not Me, But Him." If you're Martha Graham, you say to a student, "Child of God, that is *not* a *plié*!" And if you're Cliff Keuter, you create dances originating from your impressions of Idaho, because you were born and grew up there.

No matter who you think you are, if you're a real dancer, you spend many more hours sitting, standing, lying down or practicing in a room by yourself than you do performing for an audience. You spend hours faced with silence, space, light and your Self, because you don't dance with your ordinary everyday self, although that self participates in what you do when you dance.

Your 'room' may be a *manyatta* in the Maasai Mara, or a place far from other people with only cattle or sheep to see. Your 'room' may be part of a marble-floored wing of a prince's palace in New Delhi, or it may adjoin a Flamenco bar in Seville. It might be a thatched, open-sided hut in Polynesia or the adobe enclosure of a *pueblo* in New Mexico. It might be an elegant baroque *salon* somewhere in Russia or an enclosed courtyard in Japan.

Your space may be the imaginary compass upon which you stand when you practice T'ai Chi Ch'uan. No matter where your 'room' is, even if you practice with other people, you are alone because in the end, nobody makes you move. If you want to move some part of your body, say, your arm, then you have to move it. Nobody else does.

If you're a choreographer, you'd better have something to say. You'd better be able to demonstrate knowledge of your body, the silence, the space and the light, or you probably won't be able to get anyone to dance your dance. You'll do a long apprenticeship and you may discover you aren't good enough to get a job. Even if you are good enough, there might not be enough companies around who need your services.

If you don't look like a dancer according to prevailing fashions and you go through all of this simply because you want to find out more about yourself (your Self?), you're in real trouble, because, in a utilitarian, materialistic society, almost everybody wants to know why you're trying to dance when you obviously aren't cut out for it and will never make lots of money.

There are hundreds of reasons for avoiding the inner and outer spaces of a dancer, just as there are a hundred reasons for avoiding being human — even if you *are* a human being. The dancer's space, like the photographer's or the writer's (maybe all spaces), is dangerous, not, as somebody once said, because of the space itself — the 'environment' — but because *you* are dangerous.

Being human is dangerous. Living itself is dangerous because it involves risk. There are no assurances. There are tremendous hazards involved, but without them, the discoveries and above all, the growth, the *passion*, life wouldn't be worth living.

None of that stopped for me just because I hurt my left leg and my circumstances changed. I know that I never communicated my real feelings to my friend who couldn't see beyond the ruptured Achilles tendon, in spite of my attempts to explain that I never was a "dancer's dancer" so to speak. The accident I had resulted in what amounts to a potential hazard of professional dancing, as it is to high-jump skiing and long distance running. I'd been careless. I had performed without adequate warm-up out-of-doors on the concrete surface of a tennis court at a posh summer camp in Connecticut where I was Head Dance Counselor. My leg hurt badly after the performance, but I rested it and did all the things one does for muscle strain. Six weeks later, while taking a Master class in New York City, the tendon broke during a series of jumps across the floor. I was a good jumper, and the strain on an already weakened tendon was too much. The original injury wasn't "muscle strain" but torn tendon fibers.

In any case, teaching dancing had always been more important to me than performing. Performing was something I did because it was necessary, especially because I taught top-ranking professionals, both in Portland, Oregon and in New York City. Choreographing dances, although second to teaching, was more important than performing and always had been. The deep satisfaction that results from creating an entire 'mini-world' where one is in control of everything is only one thing that choreography gave to me. I've been told that performing gives this kind of satisfaction to some people, but it never did to me.

Apart from that, I was never a 'natural' as a dancer mainly because I didn't have a very good body for it and I hadn't started formal training until I was nearly thirteen. My body provided me with an excellent 'laboratory' for learning about good teaching. But performing, I hasten to say, was not a *negative* experience — I quite enjoyed it at times — it just wasn't the most important part of the process: the whole theatrical experience.

What I really wanted was to teach dancing in an enlightened fashion — to train dancers who were better dancers than I was — and do it *without injury to them*. But my efforts over the years resulted in the same situation in New York that Audrey de Vos complained about in England. My studio became a kind of informal 'hospital' for other teachers' dancers. When Lucas Hoving (a leading dancer in José Limon's company) came to me, for example, he couldn't raise his arms above shoulder height in any direction owing to severe bursitis in his shoulders. Two more special cases come to mind: José Limon himself came to me asking if I could relieve (or possibly cure) the chronic lower back pain he always felt. Liane Plane had injured herself in Agnes de Mille's *Harvest According* when she was a member of Ballet Theater. She couldn't bend over to pick up her *pointe* shoes, far less dance in them when she arrived at the studio.

After nearly two years, Liane became Chita Rivera's understudy in *West Side Story*, and ended up teaching. After eighteen months of neuro-muscular re-training, Lucas was able to dance better than he had at any other time in his career with his shoulders restored to full mobility. José and I had serious discussions about his proposed re-training because he had a choice to make: I could remove his lower back pain by realigning the hyperextended rib-cage which was characteristic of his style. But if I did that, his movement style would necessarily change. He would have to make profound alterations in his image of what moves and postures were 'masculine'. He chose to live with the pain, calling me a "back to the womb" teacher!

My reputation in New York was actually that of some kind of 'witch-doctor' who could produce results. No one really knew how it was done, therefore, not much of wider social significance came of my efforts. During those years, I taught Graham dancers how to protect themselves from a technique that tended to produce lumbar and sacroiliac problems, although for different reasons than Limon's difficulties with the same bodily area.

I taught many Humphrey-Weidman dancers how to protect themselves from knee injuries which were typical spin-offs from their technique. I taught ballet dancers how to counteract the standard, but always harmful (often idiotic) directions given in every class they took, i.e. "straighten your back" (anatomically impossible, as the spine has four curves); "turn out your knees" or "turn out your feet" (which really means rotate your legs outward from the thigh joints — the knees and feet can't rotate outward by themselves); "point your toes" (which means extend your ankles, as the toes can't 'point' on their own) and other such nonsense.

I genuinely liked this part of my work and still find it vitally interesting. To see the real potential for movement emerge out of the chaos of someone's injury and pain was certainly rewarding for them and me, but I became bored when I realized that what I taught would only have effects upon individual dancers, not upon how dance techniques were taught in the field at large. My work became boring when I finally understood that the ideas I had and the results I achieved about teaching dancing were considered by others to be purely idiosyncratic. "Too cerebral" other teachers and dancers said, because my system was based upon the relationships between spoken language, movement imagery and danced actions. Moreover, the teaching techniques I developed were generally put to use only after greater or lesser damage had been done to the person who sought my help — up to and including tipped uteruses, torn knee ligaments and spinal fusions.

I often thought of writing a book in those days and even had a title for it. In 1952, Agnes de Mille's excellent book, *Dance To The Piper*, was published. My book would be called *Pay The Piper*, but I didn't write it because I knew perfectly well that such an iconoclastic work wouldn't be welcomed — knowledge that was vindicated thirty years later when Gelsey Kirkland attempted to write a book pertaining to the dark side of the dance world.[2] People only reluctantly discover that their gods have clay feet and, for many, it is difficult (if not impossible) to change their minds. In my own case, nothing less than a ruptured Achilles tendon would have got me out of the rut my life was in, which was why I still think of it as a blessing in disguise.

My friend drove me to La Guardia Airport. A few hours later, I arrived in Minnesota where my sister met me at the airport. I was in a wheelchair. Tendons are slow to heal. I wore the boot cast and used crutches until late February 1963, but by the time the cast came off, I had passed an audition for the University of Wisconsin Dance Department as a teacher. They were impressed because I could teach a successful dance class without having to demonstrate the moves.

I was also enrolled in undergraduate courses in philosophy and aesthetics. Finally, my deep desire for higher level study was to be fulfilled! Fortunately, I had the necessary energy levels to sustain the schedule I maintained. Very soon, I found myself teaching for the University of Wisconsin Extension Division when it was in its hey-day governed by the idea of 'Wingspread' — "The borders of the state" announced the Board of Regents, "are the boundaries of the campus." The Director of the Green Bay Center, Dr. Theodore Savides (a man I greatly respected), was the first to risk offering my classes in his curriculum. I taught there and at other Centers throughout Wisconsin until I left the United States for West Africa in February 1967. Extension teaching was and still is a great joy mainly because, in that context, people study subjects because they want to learn something, not because they are busily racking up credits for a meal ticket.

---

2 Kirkland, Gelsey, with Greg Lawrence. 1986. *Dancing On My Grave : An Autobiography*. Garden City, New York: Doubleday.

As it turned out, my dancing days were not quite over. In Wisconsin, I originated a religious dance group called *Experience Anonyme*. The five people with whom I worked and I toured extensively in the upper midwest, performing in churches and helping congregations establish movement choirs. It was largely because of *Experience Anonyme* that I bought the first car I ever owned, which went from Wisconsin to Ghana with me in 1967. It was a white Volvo — the two-door model that looked like a '48 Ford. Apart from driving on church tours, the time I spent behind a steering-wheel was time spent *thinking*, especially during trips in one of the fleet of State-owned automobiles which I drove to classes in Green Bay, Racine or Janesville. The second year I worked for Extension Division, I had the unique experience of pioneering in dance therapy classes at the Wisconsin School for Girls and Taycheedah Women's Prison for the better part of a year.

In the early 'sixties, people had heard of dance therapy but only a few knew what it was all about. The warden of the School for Girls became interested in some work with movement he'd heard about that was being done in the State Hospital's psychiatric wards. He was always searching for new methods and developments that would assist rehabilitation. He approached the Vice-Chancellor of Extension Division and their discussion prompted the V.C. to ask if I might do something along therapeutic lines with dancing. I was unsure of my ability, never having attempted such work. Moreover, I wasn't too keen about the idea of using the dance as a therapeutic device, nevertheless I decided it was worth trying.

I was sure that there were identifiable features about theatrical dancing which had helped me work my way out of the emotional pain and suffering I'd endured. There was a reasonable probability that such things would help others. When the Warden asked me what I would work on with the inmates, I said, "hostility and body image." I'd done some homework: I'd learned, for example, that the problems the counseling staff in the cottages faced with the majority of girls was physical violence. They ripped bulletin boards off walls, slammed doors, slashed themselves (and each other) with pieces of broken glass from Coke bottles and dishes. They punched each other out, threw chairs across the room and in general, were destructive towards themselves and their environment.

Their sense of personal power and energy was not well directed. They didn't control their energy — they were *controlled by* their energy. They didn't know how to handle their feelings. They repressed, denied or rejected their pain. They were afraid of their energy and of their feelings because they felt they had no control. The challenge, I thought, was to teach them that they *did* have control, if they chose to exercise it.

I used techniques that I had devised for dance classes for the purpose of teaching dancers how to go through 'fight' scenes in choreographic works without hurting themselves and one another. First, I spent several sessions playing a circular game of "follow the leader" because the inmates had to get used to making the moves and assuming the postures that others did *easily* — not only the moves I made, as the authority figure in the group — but those which fellow class members performed.

One day, I came in to find them already in the circle, and I said, "OK. We're going to do something a little different today. It's a variation on a familiar theme. You're pretty good at the games we've played so far. Now, we'll do something new. I'm leader for awhile. You know how to follow."

I turned my back on the center of the circle for about ten seconds, gathering all the histrionic power I could muster, then suddenly turning towards the girl on my right, I 'mimed' hitting her such that my open hand ended about a half inch from her face. "Do it!" I shouted.

She did, imitating my action with passable fury, shouting "Do it!" and so the exercise went round the circle to the last girl, who, of course, had to perform the action towards me. She did it. The concentration, energy level and observation among the group was intense. I didn't let the flow stop.

"OK" I said, "Here's another one." Stomping towards the center of the circle, I mimed slamming a door, turned my back, stomped back to my place, slammed another door, jammed my arms into an 'akimbo' position and glared at everybody. The next girl immediately imitated the action, and the next and the next.

When it was my turn again, I lay down on the floor in a fetal position and fondled something (imaginary) I had in my hands, getting up on my knees. I hid what I had in my hands behind my back, looked around to see if anyone was watching, and then slashed at my wrists with the imaginary piece of glass, falling over as if in a faint.

By this time, the class had got onto what was happening. They entered into the whole thing with great zest and spirit. We tore bulletin boards down. We threw (imaginary) furniture. We hit one another, tripped people up, made faces and obscene gestures.

After I led the group four or five times, I could see they had the idea, so the leadership passed around the whole group. There were a dozen girls in the class. By the time they each had a turn leading, everyone was exhausted.

"Do you have anything to say?" I asked, as we sat on the floor recovering from our exertions.

"Yeah" one of them said, "When Patty stomps up to a door, she does it like this." She demonstrated. "When she did it in the dance, she didn't hit her heels hard enough on the floor."

I looked at Patty, who admitted her critic was right — and so it went.

They all wanted to play the same game next time, and asked if the 'action scenarios' could be longer. "Sure. See you day after tomorrow."

Before the next class took place, one of the girls approached me and said, "Miss, you really know what you're doing."

"Oh yeah" I retorted, "How do you know?"

"Well," she said, "last night in the cottage I got mad at the counselor and I was going to tear the bulletin board down, but you know what happened?"

"You tell me."

"I couldn't do it" she said.

"Why not?"

"Well, it was weird. I couldn't 'cause *I could see myself doing it* and it looked kind of silly, 'cause we'd done it in class."

"Wow!" I exclaimed, "You really found something out! That's terrific!"

To make a long story short, she'd discovered she had *choice*. Always before that, her blind rages precluded choices. She had no control over herself and was afraid of what she might do.

I told the Warden I didn't think people really listened to these girls, i.e. "I didn't know what I was doing" (from a girl who had stabbed her little brother with a kitchen knife, but didn't kill him); "I couldn't control myself," etc., etc. [N.B. the personal pronouns: who is the 'I' and who is 'myself' and what is the relation between the two?]

I told the warden that real performers always had to have some Self in control. If they have no control, the cast of Hamlet, for example, would end up dead every time the play was produced — and I gave other examples.

Nothing is perfect and no technique such as that described above was a panacea to all the inmates' ills, but there were a significant number of successes. "Success" is here defined by the girls who discovered that if they wanted — if they *chose* to — they could be in control of their feelings and their selves. Their intensely felt energies needn't be destructively directed. They discovered that they could do other things with the power and energy that flowed from and through them. They learned that it's all a question of who runs their internal show.

The inmates at the Wisconsin School for Girls used physical violence on themselves, others and their surroundings to keep the counseling staff (and anyone who happened to be around) off-balance. They used violence as 'proof' that their circumstances (never their responsibility, of course) were intolerable. Their often-repeated excuses for their behavior had one depressingly familiar theme: they felt *driven to act* as they did.

I quit 'therapizing' in situations like the Wisconsin School for Girls mainly because I soon realized that I was working in isolation. My 'successes' were not followed up by other staff-members, many of whom were convinced that the only value in the work I did centered in the old 'steam-valve' theory of dancing. That is, "If they perform violently in a dance class and wear themselves out, then they will be too tired to act that way in the cottages." I became disillusioned because many staff-members seemed to miss the whole point of the exercise which was about having (and making) choices. Furthermore, I was heavily involved in undergraduate course-work.

I was fortunate to have Eugene Kaelin (*The Existentialist Aesthetic*) as a beginning philosophy professor when I began my career as a student at the University of Wisconsin (Madison). Although I ultimately rejected both phenomenology and existentialism with their explanations of what human actions, dancing and life itself was all about, understanding Merleau-Ponty, Jean Paul Sartre and Heidigger became an advantage later on.

It was in connection with those early philosophy classes that I met Maxine Sheets (later, Sheets-Johnstone) who at the time was writing the only book we possess on *The Phenomenology of Dance* (University of Wisconsin Press, Madison, 1966). I learned several lessons from Maxine's experience. She was greatly upset when the dance-entertainment world and the world of dance educators produced desultory responses to her scholarly efforts. Her book dropped into limbo for the majority of dancers, choreographers and dance teachers. At the time, I found their silence difficult to understand because (naively) I believed that everyone had the same desire I did: to free the field of study from the double bind of nonliteracy and activism in which it still languishes. I couldn't believe that many dancers saw movement-writing as a threat, nor could I believe that there were those who wanted to 'experience', but had no drive to *understand* what they experienced.

It took a long time for me to adjust to the fact that the image of the "dumb dancer" and the "primitive" dancer were firmly entrenched in this country, not only in the general public's mind, but in the profession itself. If I had to identify a single source of frustration that my connection with the dance world represented over the years, it would be the notion of underestimation. There is so much more to dancing and the study of dances than most people imagine!

It is true that some people dance because they want to have fun and relax, or because they want to 'express' themselves. Some people dance because they feel sexy, happy, sad, or something. Some people dance because they want to show off or because it is an outlet for overburdened feelings. But in the end, these reasons for dancing are hopelessly superficial, even in the societies in which they are generated. They don't sufficiently explain what motivates serious professionals in the field to devote whole lifetimes to the activity.

General notions about 'entertainment', 'recreation' and 'exercise' only account for a tiny minority of the dance forms that really exist in the world. In the early 'sixties, more than anything, I wished to go somewhere in the world where dances weren't classified solely as entertainments — where people had different attitudes. I was fed up with the pervasive skepticism that says the subject lacks genuine intellectual content.

My wish was granted. The universe has ways of responding to deeply felt desire, but in its own way. I'd developed a habit of driving from Madison to New York for Christmas and Easter vacations. The Easter break, 1966, found me in Manhattan. At dinner one evening with Montego Joe (a former drummer), he suddenly pointed a finger at me during a lull in the conversation, exclaiming, "You're the one!"

"I'm the one what, Joe?" I asked, smiling, not knowing what to expect.

"You're the one Bertie Opoku is looking for," he said.

"And who's he when he's home?" I asked.

"He's an Ashanti, and he's director of the dance program at the University of Ghana" he replied. "He's looking for someone to teach western dance forms, improvisation, and that kind of stuff at the Institute of African Studies. Would you like to go there?"

"You bet I would" was my instant reply. "You know how much I'd like to study African dance forms firsthand."

About twenty minutes later, we knocked on the door of a room in the famous old Chelsea Hotel on Twenty-Third Street. A courteous Ghanaian gentleman greeted us at the door and, after an hour's visit, it was a 'done-deal'. Mr. Opoku invited me to teach at the Institute of African Studies at the University of Ghana, beginning in February 1967. I had other talks with him, and he introduced me to Seth Ladzekpo. I had no way of knowing how much Seth's home, Anyako (in the Volta region), would come to mean to me. This was largely because of an older brother of his who was a brilliant Ewe (pronounced roughly EH-vay) ritual drummer. Husunu Ladzekpo helped me immeasurably during the three and a half years I was to live in Ghana.

To some extent, during the rest of my stay in New York, I felt as if I were living in a dream-world. My emotional state could be described as 'ecstatic' — and I left the city two days earlier than I'd planned because I had so much to do and think about now that my wish to go to a country where attitudes towards dancing were very different was to come true. My mind raced: who would take over my classes, and so forth in Wisconsin? What would I take with me and what would I leave behind?

Providence had smiled on me: the 'loaf of bread' that day brought with it in New York was to change my life yet again, but in ways I wouldn't have believed had anyone told me how events would unfold during the time I would live in West Africa. Ten years later, in 1976, I wrote:

> Three-and-a-half years in Ghana taught me much. I came from there an altered person, but one significant impression stands out as a result of the fieldwork done there. It consists of ". . . the daily experience of not knowing" (Edwin Ardener - lectures).
>
> While in Ghana my main concern was with learning some Ghanaian dances and attempting to absorb, insofar as I was then capable, elements of societies quite different from my own. The interest in West African dance had been awakened some years before, through intensive study with Pearl Primus and Percival Borde in New York City between 1956 and 1961. I arrived in Ghana having had extensive study and performing experience in four idioms of dance, three years of undergraduate philosophy and aesthetics, many years of teaching experience — and boundless energy and enthusiasm.
>
> It would be difficult to assess, now, which was the greater; the enthusiasm or my naïveté. Both, fortunately were exceeded by

the patience, generosity and hospitality of my many teachers of dancing in several parts of Ghana and the Ivory Coast. If truth in communication had depended entirely on their good will, there would be no need to write this essay. If the accuracy of verbal reports of danced events and experience depended solely on the desire to learn or the willingness to teach, there would be few, if any, problems of communication. But as I tried to learn from them and tried to record the dance events in which I participated, I slowly realized that I did not know how to translate any of the experience — my own or theirs — into any other terms or any other system or mode of expression (Williams 1991[1976]: 291).[3]

On the morning of February 17, 1967, startled awake out of a sound sleep by a chorus of rasping (but not unmelodious) croaks from a big population of frogs, all of which seemed to be situated under the open windows of my room in the University's guest house, I was innocently unaware of the size and extent of the cultural baggage I brought to West Africa with me.

In the distance, accompanying the frogs, I thought I heard the beating of drums.

---

[3] See 'An Exercise in Applied Personal Anthropology' (Appendix 1) in Williams, Drid. 1991. *Ten Lectures on Theories of the Dance*. Metuchen, New Jersey: Scarecrow Press, pp. 287-321.

Chapter 12

> It's not just what we inherit from our mothers and fathers that haunts us. It's all kinds of old defunct theories, all sorts of old defunct beliefs, and things like that. It's not that they actually live on in us; they are simply lodged there ...
> (Henrik Ibsen, *Ghosts*, 1881, Act 2).

I was too excited to sleep. The choir of frogs and birdsong was an excuse to venture out-of-doors to greet my first West African morning. Attracted first towards the rear of the guesthouse, I saw men and women cooking both in a kitchen and on an open fire on a cement patio outside the kitchen door. An 'English breakfast' for guests was in preparation in the kitchen. A deliciously fragrant stew bubbling in an iron pot hanging from a tripod over the fire was Ghanaian fare in preparation for the mid-day meal. "*Akwáába, akwáába*" [ah-KWAHB-ah], ("Welcome") they said in *Twi* [TWEE] (the Ashanti language).

"Thank you, thank you" I replied, too shy and unsure of myself to answer as someone briefly tried to teach me to do the night before at an orientation party for new arrivals at the Institute of African Studies. I was much more interested in seeing how the sounds originated from what I mistook to be drums. Women were pounding *fou-fou*[1] — the rhythms of their activity echoing near and far from every bungalow on the university grounds.

In its edible, finished form, *fou-fou* forms a soft round, or oblong, off-white loaf from which bits are taken by the thumb, index and second finger of the right hand, dipped adroitly into a stew and carried to the mouth. Its texture is somewhat like a cross between semolina pudding and mashed potato: its taste bland, like potato, but pleasing. *Fou-fou* is made from one of the twenty-four varieties of yam that grow in Ghana, none of them like the sweet, orange-fleshed tuber that so enhances American

---

1 Literally translated, *fou-fou* is 'white-white'.

Thanksgiving tables. Yams in Ghana can be eight to twelve inches long and an inch and a half in diameter, ranging upwards in size to immense tubers reaching two or three feet in length and five to seven inches across. Their flesh ranges from chalk-white (the biggest ones) to shades of white tinged with delicate hues of rose or yellow.

I've seen the giant variety stacked like cordwood on an old World War II landing barge which was used as a ferry across the Volta River. The yams enclosed three of the barge's open sides like the eight-foot high walls of a room. I stood near the yams, savoring the smell of rich black earth still clinging to their leathery brown exteriors. On the barge, aisles were formed by the yam-walls and the sides of my Volvo, but they were narrow aisles, because they were crammed with pushcarts, crates of chickens, baskets of garden produce and children. The children were accompanied by an assortment of adults and two or three goats. River-crossings to Ketekrachi (in 1967, the Volta Dam was not yet built) were colorful, noisy, hour-long 'holidays'![2]

For meals, the big yams are first hacked into manageable pieces with a *machete* [meh-SHET-ay], then washed, peeled and tossed into a pot to boil. The cooled cooked chunks are placed, a few at a time, in the bottom of a big wooden vessel — a mortar-like receptacle (often the hollowed-out section of a small tree-trunk). The yam is then pounded with a four-and-a-half-foot long pestle about five inches in diameter held in both hands of a woman whose body straightens and bends from the waist, as she brings her whole body weight to bear on the bottom of the mortar and its contents — BOM!; S-w-i-s-h— BOM!; S-w-i-s-h— BOM!; S-w-i-s-h— BOM!

As the woman with the big stick straightens her body, her companion (usually a younger woman) sitting on a three-legged stool, deftly reaches into the bottom of the vessel with her right hand and "turns" the yam chunks, sometimes adding water, a little milk, maybe, or she oils her hand (if oil is available).

---

2 The Volta River eventually flows into the sea in eastern Ghana through a delta in *Ewe* (EH-vay) country, finally to empty into the Gulf of Guinea.

Heaven help the maladroit whose attention wanders or who isn't into the rhythm of the task! But accidents rarely if ever happen, because yam-pounding is accompanied by soft singing.

In the early morning in any of the southern villages in Ghana — as in every compound on the university grounds on my first day — the women make *fou-fou*. Small wonder I thought there was drumming going on, for the muffled sounds of many pestles, not occurring in unison (each woman has her own style and rhythm of pounding), accompanied by *a cappella* singing, easily sounds to the untutored ear like drumming. But, nearly everything I saw and heard in Ghana was new to me.

At the welcoming party the previous night, I both saw and heard startling things. For example, good manners in Ghana (as in the United States) demand that upon meeting a man you know is married, you inquire about the health and well-being of his wife. Introduced to Professor Kwabena Nketia (an eminent, internationally known musicologist, then the Director of the Institute of African Studies), I did what my culture and upbringing required of me.

"And how is your wife, Professor?"

"Which one?" he asked, with twinkling eyes.

It was thus I learned that I had taken up residence for some time to come in a polygynous, not a monogamous, society. I was embarrassed, to say the least!

I'd also noticed differences in how people greeted one another in my new home, although Ghanaians shake hands with one another more or less as Americans do. Since movement, dances and gesture were my primary interest, I perceived many small but significant things. At cocktail parties, for instance, Americans tend to hold their drinks in their left hands, leaving their right hands free to shake hands. If they are holding a plate of *hors d'oeuvres*, rendering both hands unavailable, they will find someplace to put plate or glass down, freeing their right hands. Some of the Ghanaians I met had different solutions.

When I reached my hand toward one gentleman with his hands full, he offered his right forearm for me to clasp or touch. Some of my hosts shook my right hand with theirs in an expected way, but they supported their right elbows with their left hands while doing so, bowing slightly from the waist. When I met the young woman who was turning the *fou-fou* in the morning outside the guest house, she gracefully placed her right forearm near the elbow on top of her left forearm offering me her left hand to clasp. There were numerous variations on the standard handshake with which I was familiar.

The most complicated greeting ceremony I experienced occurred in Lawra, Ghana (Lobi country) two months later, when I was greeted by Charles Deri's[3] father, Dikpe [DIK-pay] at his compound, which covered the same area as approximately half an American city block. Travelling on my first research trip with three of the Institute's students, I had been alerted beforehand about Lobi greeting ceremonies so I could conduct myself in an appropriate manner.[4]

It was just before dusk when we arrived. Charles's six-foot tall father came striding towards me across the rooftops of the huge compound, his beautiful toga-like dress-cloth billowing behind him. That far north, people not only sleep on the roof in special sleeping mats because of the heat, they gather under the stars in the cool of the evening to eat, converse and take their ease after a day's work. I awaited him, both arms full of three large-size yams, a bottle of Beefeater's gin, a dozen candles in a box, a carton of box matches, and a hunting knife I'd brought as a gift especially for him. When he stretched his right hand towards me, I knelt (as Charles had told me that was the signal to kneel and place the gifts between him and me), after which I looked up at him and offered him my right hand — still kneeling.

Mr. Deri took my hand, speaking several paragraphs of greeting in *Losssale* [Loh-SOL-ay] which Charles translated.

---

3 Charles Deri was a student at the Institute of African Studies; one of three who accompanied me on the trip to Lawra. Another student's name was Roland Harunnah, whose aunt was our hostess in Bolgatanga. Seth Kumah, the third student, was from Ketekrachi.

4 Lawra is in the northwest quadrant of Ghana, 511 miles north and 150 miles west of Accra [ah-CRAW], the national capitol near the southern coast.

During the few seconds I dealt with getting the yams and other gifts into a neat pile, he had moved to his father's right, standing as the point of a triangle facing us. I replied to his father (still kneeling), extending greetings to his household with special mention of his father and mother and their wives and husbands, Mr. Deri's wives, his wives' brothers and their wives, and, finally, his brothers and *their* wives. "Extended family" indeed! Still kneeling, I asked permission to visit his house, expressing sorrow that my gifts were so poor for so fine a man with such a great family.

He replied by raising me to a standing position, shaking my hand, which he let go in order to signal to one of the twenty-odd people who had followed him at the required respectful distance of about ten yards behind. Three of them instantly moved forward. The first, a man, gave me three yams tied together in a bundle exactly like those I had brought. I took those in my right hand. The second, a woman (Sulu, the first wife) gave me a beautiful hand-woven basket decorated with cowrie shells that contained a dozen guinea fowl eggs. I transferred the yam-bundle from right to left hand and took the basket with my right. The third (another man) offered me a live cockerel which I subsequently took back to Accra. Since I had managed to shift the basket to my left hand, now holding the yams under my left arm, I took the rooster with my right hand. Turning to my right, I looked at Roland Harunnah (the second student who accompanied me) who came forward relieving me of the gifts I had been given. He stood on my right, facing Charles. Seth Kumah (the third student) stood behind me at a distance trying to look important enough to balance the *entourage* that Mr. Deri had with him.

Turning back to face my host, I again shook hands with Mr. Deri, who conducted me to the group waiting behind him, where he proceeded to introduce each of them. I knew by that time to start with the person on my right, moving across the assembled company towards the left. I did this because that way, the palm of my right hand faced each of them. Had I started on the left and moved towards the right, I would have been giving them "the back of my hand" as it were, which wasn't considered polite. After the greetings were over, we were served with *Pito* [PEE-toh] (a kind of wine made from guinea corn and fermented with yeast) by Charles's new wife, Milnibe [MILL-nee-beh]. The *Pito* got stronger as the evening advanced, but we had food, and we retired fairly early. The journey from Bolgatonga had been long and tiring.

The upshot of all this is that from the earliest days of residence in Ghana, I realized that one's body isn't the same in West Africa as it is in one's home country. Of course, I don't mean that one's physical body or physical *persona* changes. One's social body — the *social persona* changes into the defining framework with its resulting demeanors that are compatible with the concepts of the host-people. In Ghana, the spatial dimensions of right and left — as extensions of the right and left sides of one's body — are of fundamental importance.

The right hand isn't merely a biological object that is more or less symmetrical with the left. The assigned social values of right and left hands are assymmetrical — as they are throughout the world. In Ghana (as in India and many other places) the right hand is (socially) clean. The left hand is (socially) unclean. One eats with one's right hand in contrast to cleaning one's self after using the toilet, which is something *only* the left hand does. The woman pounding *fou-fou* has both hands on the pestle, but her right hand is placed *above* the left. The woman turning the *fou-fou* never turns it with her left hand. With regard to many acts, however, one is permitted to transform the left hand into the right by touching the left forearm with the right-hand or forearm, thus making it acceptable to offer someone an object with, or to shake, the left hand.

From the beginning in mid-February, 1967, until I left in August 1970, my life was a constant process of learning which often involved, as I later wrote, "the painful collapse of long established, firmly believed-in parameters of social interaction, models of reality and the world, moral and behavioral 'laws', etc." The first major belief to 'hit the dust' so to speak, was about the universality of the meanings of movement. Like everyone else, I knew about the language barrier and that spoken languages had to be translated, but (perhaps like many others), I thought I could rely on my knowledge of movement not only to communicate but *really* to understand what was going on around me. It took a long time for the myth of the universality of movement's semantics to topple, largely because dancing was my speciality. However, from the first dance class I taught the second week I was in Ghana, that myth started to erode until, by the time I left the country, there was nothing left of it! The best way of explaining what I mean is through re-telling two anecdotes, both of which I wrote to Doris in Minnesota.

THE DANCE CLASS

Imagine a large, empty studio space (75' x 110') with ballet barres on three sides, interrupted only by double doors permitting entry on both long sides of the rectangle. At the 'free-end' of the room is a mobile blackboard, a desk, an odd chair or two, a coat-hanger, tape-recording equipment and some boxes. Entering this space at eight o'clock Monday morning (the last week in February), I went to the blackboard-end of the room and, finding myself alone, sat down in one of the chairs to wait. Class was scheduled for 8:15 a.m.

Promptly at the appointed time, twenty-three young men entered the studio through the double-doors on the left side of the room. They didn't straggle in. They came in together, went directly to the center of the studio and stood facing me all in a 'clump', so to speak. They stood very close together. This was unlike anything I'd experienced in any class I'd ever taught but, I thought, "I'm new to them, so I'll start with a greeting."

"*Akwáába, akwáába*" I said, and they replied in kind, smiling, welcoming me. There was silence.

"I'm Professor Williams" I announced, "and will you please take space, as I want to begin the class."

"Take space" meant they were supposed to stand at least a full arm's-length apart from one another in staggered lines (so that I could see each student), filling the room according to a kind of prearranged ranking system, prevalent among dance students in America: the best students stand in front so that everyone can copy them; the least accomplished students occupy the back of the room.

Nothing happened, except that the group continued to smile at me, and they all bowed.

I bowed back, deciding to try again: "Take space" I ordered, spreading my arms wide, hoping to communicate what I wanted by doing so.

They looked at one another. I saw four or five puzzled faces among the twenty-three, and they bowed again, as one man.

"Good heavens!" I thought to myself, "They don't know what I mean. Now what do I do?" Smiling at them, I walked slowly towards the group until I was about four feet from the foremost members of the clump. Dancer-like, I sank to the floor. They instantly imitated my action.

Explaining that I was going to teach American modern dance classes, I told them that these classes had a certain spatial form they were meant to learn along with the exercises I would teach. I spelled out what "take space" meant.

Asking them to remain on the floor, I got up and pulled the blackboard to the center of the room and drew diagrams. Satisfied that I had accomplished the purpose, I told them to go back to the double doors where they had entered, saying we would start all over again.

This time, when I said "take space" they distributed themselves throughout the room as required, but they looked very uncomfortable in their individual spatial islands. As they later explained, they felt estranged from one another: the ones in front couldn't see what the people behind them were doing. Those in the back row complained that they couldn't see me very well. We struggled through the hour-and-a-half class that morning, but the next day, I promised we would try something different.

Indeed, I said, "I want you to teach me how you stand and what you do when you learn." My suggestion was agreeable, and that's how we proceeded: I taught them and in turn, they taught me. To this day, I'm positive that I benefited far more than they did from those classes. In the end, the 'form' the class took was a compromise: I stood in the middle of the studio-space. They arranged themselves around me in loose, concentric circles.

THE NEW HOUSE

When I moved out of the guest-house in March 1967, I wasn't alone in my new university bungalow. I had a cook-steward, acquired through the able assistance of one of the Institute staff: an Englishwoman (an old Africa-hand), who "knew the ropes." I protested strongly about having house-help, but finally capitulated, mainly because of the language-argument.

"How are you going to shop for food?" she asked. "Nobody in the market speaks English (except pidgin-English) and most of the day-to-day trading here is done in Hausa — the language of the markets. You don't know how to bargain" she said, "*Everybody* bargains for *everything* in Ghana and if you don't know how, you will be taken for a very expensive ride! Moreover, it's expected that Europeans will have Africans looking after them. Apart from anything else, it contributes to the local economy."

"I'm not European" I said rebelliously, knowing full well that all white people were called that in West Africa regardless of their national origin.

She looked at me with ill-concealed exasperation: "Well, Professor Nketia [nnn-KET-yah] told me to look over some people who want work, and I think I've found the ideal person for you. His name is David Akele [ah-KAY-lay]. He's Nigerian, an excellent cook and housekeeper, and he knows exactly what to do."

Over the next few months, I realized that David *did* know exactly what to do and I did not. Worse yet, I'd never had a servant, and I didn't know how to behave. Most of the activities I was accustomed to performing in my own home were taken over by David, who put up with my inexperience and *gaucherie* with remarkable aplomb. British and American friends tried to be helpful, explaining that the whole point of the exercise was that I was to do *nothing* — not my laundry, the cleaning, or the cooking or buying of food. In sum, I was to leave running the household entirely to him.

"Just stay out of his way" friends told me. "He'll manage." And he did. It was a hard lesson to learn in one's late 'thirties — I felt bereft of half my reason-for-being — but it wasn't too long before I got used to a life without housework and liked it very much. For the first time, I discovered how many men were used to living! Like many women my age, I'd been a cook-steward for two husbands.

David was from the River States in Nigeria. He was at least fifteen years older than I, and he was a fine cook — West African or 'European' dishes. He prepared fish that was more delicious than any I'd ever had and he liked the fact that I wanted to sample West African foods, often asking him to serve native Nigerian or Ghanaian dishes when I entertained dinner guests. He didn't like having me in the kitchen when he prepared meals, so I never learned his recipes, more's the pity! He liked the fact that I'm a fairly tidy person, therefore not too hard to look after because I didn't leave my things around or make messes in the house, but he didn't like the fact that I had no husband or children with me.[5]

David spoke 'proper' (as opposed to 'broken', also called 'pidgin') English very well, but most of his friends who came occasionally to visit him only spoke pidgin English. One day in April while convalescing at home after a week in the university hospital following the trip to Lawra, I heard David telling a friend the story of what happened to me, which I recorded.

> Madam go be sick. Madam go for trek. 'E go for long way to Lawra. She go for dance, she de write. She write plenty. 'E be heem drive for long-way. When 'e go to Lawra 'e be eemself cook, 'e be eemself write, 'e be eemself drive — he be eemself do every t'ing.
>
> Which kind person he go fit do so? 'E be strong woman. Me I no savvy. She no know de water be dirty — no be good — and she no clean de pan proper and she no make de chop fine.[6]

---

5 He wasn't alone. I finally invented a family and a plausible reason in West African terms for leaving them in the U.S. while I travelled. I had Doris send some snapshots of Dorian and I carried pictures of my cousin's four children.

6 'Chop' means food — dinner; or any meal.

Dat's why de Doctor say plenty yamma-yamma[7] come trouble 'e.

So de Doctor say next time you go, go make you take somebody on your cook way - 'e go cook for you. De t'ing the cook savvy, Madam no savvy. Be chop way Madam go chop, way go good for her. Me I savvy. Madam 'e no know *a'tall*!

'E be stranger and 'e no savvy. What 'e do will be foolish t'ings.

Seeing pidgin English on a printed page gives some impression of the rhythm and the intonation of it. Sad to say, it doesn't convey any of the lovely sounds, gestures or color that accompanies it. David taught me broken English, because without this *folk-talk* of Ghana, you can't converse with traders, market women or anyone, really, except university people. After I became somewhat proficient, there were days David and I didn't speak anything else at home. A typical conversation about the fact there were no groceries in the house went like this:

DV: "What you go chop dis night?"

DR: "What you go make I like-um."

DV: "Madam, we no get proper t'ing for house."

DR: "No meat for freeze?"

DV: "Madam, nothin' dey in-si-oh" [inside].

DR: "Nothin' dey insi' de fridge *a'tall*? Me, I no believe so. Today be two days I buy some meat I bring-ah. Which side de meat go?"

DV: "Madam, I cook and finish."

DR: "Just now I de write. I no fit go out. Take de money. Go buy some meat ... na be only meat. What again we like we will buy."

DV: "Madam, we go buy chicken, anything you mean to put in ... I go buy vegetable, paw-paw ... like dat."

DR: "All right. (Handing him money). Take-um. If you go, come back-a-quick.

DV: "Yes, Madam."

---

7 This refers to any illness, but in my case it was suppressed malaria, an acute attack of amoebic dysentery (fortunately not the chronic variety) and bile-duct and gall-bladder infections from drinking unboiled water. All were complicated by exhaustion.

David stayed with me for about eighteen months, until I came back from a field trip to Ketekrachi with Father Hans Steemers at the end of June, 1968. When I returned, he had disappeared. Nobody seemed to know where he had gone, or if they did, they weren't telling me. I finally tracked him down at his new employer's compound some distance from the university and found out that he left because he didn't like the relationship I had with Mustapha Tettey Addy, one of many drummers at the Institute, who accompanied me nearly everywhere after the initial field trip to Lawra.[8]

Addy ended up occupying one of the spare bedrooms in the bungalow starting in September 1967, but David considered it improper for Addy to live in my house: he resented cooking and cleaning for him, although Addy did his own laundry. Unbeknownst to me and owing to Addy's presence in the house, I gradually fell farther and farther into disrepute with David because I had crossed social barriers that to him were unbridgeable.

There were other problems, too: David was short and had obviously had rickets as a child, making him slightly bow-legged, with a head, hands and feet that looked too large for his body. Addy was well-proportioned: tall, lithe and very good-looking. David made good money as my cook-steward, but Addy made more money and received more gifts as my research assistant than David made. To make matters worse, Addy was Muslim and David was a professed Christian. The final insult, adding to increased feelings of injury, was that David was Addy's senior in age.

---

8 Addy later came to England, and, using the 800 cubic feet of drums and instruments I took there with me, made an LP record: *Mustapha Tettey Addy, Master Drummer of Ghana*, available on the Lyrichord label in the United States. He later made another record with some of his brothers who came to England when they all drummed for the ill-fated Munich Olympics. That record was called *Kpanlogo* [PAN-LOGO] *Party*.

Chapter 13

> I have lost friends, some by death ...
> others by sheer inability to cross the street.
> (*The Waves*, Virginia Woolf, p. 202).

When I first met Addy, he was merely one of several drummers at the Institute of African Studies who was also a member of the Ghana Dance Ensemble. He soon became an indispensable interpreter/assistant as he had a natural gift for language-learning and could converse in *Ewe*, *Fanti*, *Twi* and English apart from his native language, Ga [GAH]. He was a magnificent drummer, who, according to Husunu Ladzekpo, could "drum like an Ewe." Coming from the senior master drummer in Eweland, that was an accolade!

He was the only master drummer (including Husunu) among the many I met in Ghana who was equally as proficient on *Ewe*, *Ashanti* and *Fanti* drums and gongs as he was on his own *Ga* instruments. He also played *dondo*: the West African squeeze-drum, one of the many "talking" drums of Ghana, widely used in the north. But his versatility as a drummer was a prize he'd won that cost him dearly later on in two major ways.

He learned most of the drumming he knew in Accra's *Zongo* — the part of town where Ghanaian new arrivals from outlying districts and immigrants from other West African countries lived. Addy spent nearly all of his time there during his primary school years instead of going to school. He played hooky so that he could learn drumming, singing and dancing. Later on, of course, he longed to be literate — it cost him a lot to tell me, the first time the occasion arose, that he couldn't read. But, by the time I left Ghana in August 1970, he could read and write because we spent many hours working on the skills he had missed by not going to school.

The second price Addy paid during the time I was in Ghana (and later, when he came to England) had to do with our relationship and with his age. We never knew exactly how old

Addy was because his birth-year was surrounded by doubt, but he elicited whatever information that was available. As nearly as we could work things out, we reckoned he was about twenty-seven years old — give or take a year or two in either direction.

He was married six years before we met and had a little boy, but he lived apart from his wife who felt she couldn't join him when he became Muslim. I never knew which meant more to Addy: his faith in Islam or his drumming. I didn't push the question, even when I was up at three in the morning out in the bush somewhere cooking a pre-dawn meal for him in preparation for a day of fasting during the Ramadan. Two of the dances we researched in Nafana country (western Ivory Coast) only took place once a year during Ramadan, because the Nafana year was reckoned according to a lunar calendar. He fasted during the three trips we made to study the Bedu Dance.[1]

The fact that I was at least eleven years older than Addy didn't matter to his family or to most of the Ghanaians he knew. To his senior brother, Yacubu (also a drummer at the Institute), it made all the difference, even to the extent that, to his senior brothers and many Ghanaians, Addy didn't even deserve to be called a 'master' drummer. He wasn't old enough to be worthy of that title. As his senior in age, Yacubu felt that he should have had the privilege of living and working with me — not Addy.

My cook-steward, David, agreed with Yacubu. He was of the opinion that Addy was simply too young to do (and to be and have) the things he did. Apart from anything else, Addy was deemed too young to make the kind of money he made working with me. Because of his relationship with me, he was too young to be "put over senior men's heads in your house" as David put it. That is, the closeness of our relationship and the fact that Addy lived in my house effectively made him the master of the house both to David and to many casual observers.

At the time, I became frequently irritated by those who, in spite of overwhelming evidence to the contrary, still held to the romantic notion of an alleged natural primitive life that was

---

[1] See 1968. 'The Dance of the Bedu Moon'. *African Arts/arts d'Afrique*, Los Angeles: University of California.

assumed to have no social rules of conduct, thus embodying a dream of freedom from civilized constraint. The romanticized fantasy of the so-called "noble savage" (which I'm sure Rousseau himself wouldn't recognize) turned out to be solely the product of an European imagination. First in Ghana, then in Aboriginal Australia, later in Kenya, the knowledge I gained watching indigenous friends struggle with rigid traditional con-cepts of birth order, age grades and seniority, convinced me that human beings, far from being free in traditionally oriented non-literate contexts, were more hedged about with behavioral sanctions than those in industrialized societies.

Nevertheless, David didn't like having Addy live in my house, nor did he care for hearing me referred to as "Addy's woman." He never really knew whether Addy and I slept together (in my view, nobody's business but Addy's and mine), but tongues wagged endlessly. There was much speculation, not only among Ghanaians, but among the so-called 'European' community regarding the nature of our relationship. I found that *obrunis* (the plural of the *Ga* word, *obruni*, or 'white person') were divided along predictable lines: those to whom sexual relationships between Africans and non-Africans didn't matter remained my friends. Those to whom real or imagined sexual relationships *did* matter became distant and cool. Unlike Virginia Woolf, I didn't lose some friends because of their "sheer inability to cross the street," but because of their inability to cross racial barriers.

To a large extent, I was a marginal person with regard to the European community anyway because I was single, divorced and a dancer. Perhaps more important, I was a 'nobody' having no economic or political clout whatsoever. Had I been independently wealthy, a member of the diplomatic community, a normal University faculty member and/or married, the response to Addy's and my relationship would have been different. Indeed, there probably wouldn't have been a close relationship at all. As it was, during my stay in Ghana, I enjoyed the tolerance of *laissez-faire* from the European community in whatever I chose to do. My activities were classified as 'personal', and because they had no lasting effects upon anyone, I suffered very little from the community's good intentions and caring.

English friends enjoyed the meals they ate at my table — often tasting West African cuisine for the first time. But, they expected an American to "go native"; something the Brits almost never did. There were notable exceptions like the Englishman, whose name I don't remember, who was the acknowledged chief of a branch of a local tribe. They often joked about my job, which to them was "carrying coals to Newcastle" (teaching dancing in a country known for its many dances, and to Africans, who presumably can dance whatever else they might or might not be able to do).

On the whole, American friends weren't any more interested in my private life than my Anglo-European compatriots were. They were interested in the research I did and the essays I wrote and managed to get published about Ghanaian dances. Both groups were genuinely interested, I think, in what I came to know about an area that was as foreign to them in their own cultures as it was in Ghana. Those who weren't interested in dancing or in the research I carried out were relatively superficial acquaintances whom I knew because we were occasionally thrown together at meetings or parties.

Without exception, the *obrunis* who did maintain regular and frequent contact with me loved Addy. Without exception, they greatly respected his extraordinary talent. Moreover, he made a lot of money drumming for them on various occasions but, among his family and many colleagues at the Institute, his financial good fortune was a source of bitter envy and jealousy.

Among other things, Addy helped his mother and supported his son with the money he made, but I never knew exactly how much of the money he made found its way into other family members' pockets. He hated the fact that his drumming couldn't be judged by his brothers on its own merits rather than his age. He was often angry or in despair over the relentless badgering he took over money. There was very little — actually nothing — I could do to assist, as I was the source of his good fortune and therefore, of his brothers' discontent.

Some of the pressure was relieved when, owing to the financial support and the efforts of a remarkable and enlightened African-American woman, Shirley Quarmyne, we were able to start a small, although short-lived, performing company known by the Ewe name *Adzido* (meaning the strength of a great tree in terms of its application to the group) for which Husunu Ladzekpo drummed, and several members of the Institute's Ensemble danced.[2]

Thanks to Mrs. Quarmyne's patronage, *Adzido* performed the relatively few times it did with authentic costumes, instruments, etc. from every area we represented: *Ewe, Ga, Dagomba,* and *Fanti* to start, with plans to add more areas as time went on. Needless to say, perhaps, the company was not welcomed by the Institute of African Studies, in particular, by Mr. Opoku who became an enemy. The main bone of contention was the Ewe *Agbekɔ* about which I wrote years later.[3] The Ghana Dance Ensemble's performance of the dance didn't resemble anything that actually was performed in the areas in eastern Ghana where it could still be seen.

> When I saw the Ewe *Agbekɔ* dance in the Volta Region ... I didn't see anything at first: I heard the drums from a distance, then I saw the procession of drummers and dancers slowly approaching the cleared dance space. The first time I saw *Atsimivu* [the Ewe master drum] it was carried on a drum-bearer's head, and Husunu, his chest bare (out of respect for the occasion and the import of the dance) with a *kente* cloth wrapped around his waist so that it covered his lower body, was drumming as he walked, following *Atsimivu*, which was preceded by Sogo and the gong, then followed by the other supporting drums, after which the male dancers, then the female dancers appeared. The processional form was used, I was told, because the old dance, out of which *Agbekɔ* was formed, was done when the men returned home from wars. The women ran out to meet them, and this kind of procession was the result. The procession continued around

---

[2] I later documented at least one of the performing efforts of this group in an essay entitled, 'Traditional Danced Spaces. Concepts of *Deixis* and the Staging of Non-Western Dances' in the *International Journal of African Dance*, Vol. 1, No. 2, Fall, 1994, pp. 8-20.

[3] The phonetic symbol 'ɔ' is pronounced somewhat like the English word, 'awe', therefore the name of this dance is (roughly) AG-beh-kaw. It is virtually impossible to translate the word, but it means something like "life goes on."

the cleared dance space, then the drummers took up their position, the dancers continuing until they faced the master drum, thus establishing the major line of action (Williams 1994: 13).

I didn't understand why Opoku staged the dance the way he did, which was counter to variations on the visual themes I have described. The many acrimonious discussions we had over the staging of Agbekɔ nearly always started when he said his version of the staging was the way it was because of the shape of a western proscenium stage. Invariably, he pointed out that

[A]ll the movements were Ewe movements and that the steps and drum beats were accurate. I agreed with that (with only a few reservations), but said that I didn't think that all there was to a dance was the movements and steps which it included. He said I wasn't an African and, therefore, had no business saying anything about it at all. I said, "You may be an African—specifically, a Ghanaian—but you're an Ashanti, you're not Ewe, therefore, why do you think you know any more about it than I do?" He disdained to answer (Williams 1994: 14).

I asked him if he had seen Agbekɔ in the field. He said, "Yes," so I asked, "Did it start with a procession?"

"Yes, it did."

"But then why don't you stage it that way?"

"Because I think the procession is boring. Nobody wants to watch that, so I changed it."

"Oh. Did you change the line of the dance and the groupings of the dancers because you found those boring too?"

"No, I don't have enough dancers who know the Ewe patterns well enough to do all those [traditionally required] solos and duets."

"But you have enough Ewe dancers to teach the others what they are supposed to do, don't you?"

"You really make me disgusted," he said, "the Ewe dance isn't the only one we do. I can't spend that much time on it. Besides that, the way I stage these dances is the way that will please foreigners. I studied modern dance in New York. I went to the Rockefeller Center. I know what they like to see. Actually, I think I know what's bothering you: you're one of those preservation freaks. You can't put palm trees, huts, chickens, goats, dust and everything on stage. You want to recreate the village on the stage." I told him he was wrong, but didn't expect him to believe me.

In fact, looking back on those conversations now, it amuses me to think about how credulous I was. My participation in *Adzido* was based on the assumption that if Opoku could see a more traditionally accurate staging of the dances than his Ensemble did and see how well-received *Adzido's* work was, that his own staging would change.

It's hard to believe that I was actually convinced of that, but I was. At the time, it seemed to me that Opoku staged traditional dances the way he did because he was ignorant of staging the work any other way. It took me a long time to learn that his division between self-interest and artistic values is a view that has been held for a long time in the modern world. It was my view of these matters that was (and still is) out-of-date. But, it's an ethical question, and I remember thinking a lot about Socrates — not that I was asked to drink hemlock in Ghana in order to remove my corrupting influence from the students at the Institute of African Studies. Instead, Prof. Nketia gracefully suggested that I teach dancing at the Teachers' Training College in Winneba west of Accra on the coast in *Fanti* territory. Winneba was far enough away from the University to satisfy Mr. Opoku, who by August 1968 regretted asking me to come to Ghana at all. But I had a contract, and it was fulfilled, although not all of it at the University of Ghana.

I was as glad to leave the Institute of African Studies as my former boss was to see me go. I needed time-out from the heavy schedule of rehearsals, classes, etc. in which I became involved not only because I wanted to do more field research, but because I really hated the altercations that arose over the rival dance company Mrs. Quarmyne had started. It was impossible for me to choreograph and direct *Adzido* from Winneba, so I was able to bow out tactfully, hoping the group could continue on its own or with someone who would try to maintain the integrity of traditional spatial forms in performance as I had done. Most of all, I needed time to think about my life and what I was doing with it.

Winneba was a perfect place to accomplish the new goal. My teaching schedule was considerably lighter and the atmosphere at the Training College was totally unlike that of the University. Not surprisingly, the most striking difference of which I was aware was the attitude towards traditional dancing. I only attempted to teach the traditional dances I had learned once or twice during my stay at the College, because none of the students there wanted to learn it. There were serious complaints to the Principal of the College from Ashantis about learning *Ewe* movements and from *Ewes* about learning *Ga* movements, for example. None of the students wanted to learn any other group's dances.

They wanted to learn Foxtrot, Waltz, Tango, Samba — all of the western dances they had seen in films — and that is what I taught during my six months residence in Winneba. I made some half-hearted attempts to argue, but soon gave up. As one young man put it, "Why do I want to learn those dances? I know my own, and have to perform (he was a chief's son) on appropriate occasions in my village to please the people. Other than that, I'm not interested. I want to know things that will advance me in European society."

I disliked the Winneba students' attitudes intensely, but who was I to try to change them? It seemed that I'd come to West Africa only to end up teaching American ballroom dancing. I could make considerably more money doing that in the United States. As I didn't want to pack everything in and leave Ghana, I simply 'marked time' in Winneba. I learned what I could about local customs. I enjoyed being able to buy a small bucket of avocados (four or five) for the equivalent of twenty-five cents. I combined these with fresh lobster tails and grapefruit — an unbeatable combination arranged on a bed of lettuce. The food was fabulous: paw-paw, oranges, African spinach, fresh fish of all kinds and descriptions, and my cook-steward (although not so accomplished as David) produced lovely meals. I organized the research I'd done, thought a lot about where I'd been and where

I was going, and I relaxed — probably for the first time since arriving in Ghana.

Although Addy visited me from time to time, he remained in Accra, and his problems with his family and Adzido faded into the background of my existence. My main confidante during this time was a man who was then the Catholic Chaplain at the University — Father Han Steemers — a Dutch priest who was a member of the S.M.A. (Societe des Missionnaires d'Afrique in Rome).

Father Steemers and I traveled together several times to Ketekrachi in eastern Ghana, some miles north of the coast, to the area that was to be flooded out by the lake which would be created when the Volta Dam was sealed up. The Krachi [KRAW-chee] and Ntwumuru [n-n-CHOO-mer-oo] peoples were undergoing government-sponsored relocation, as their villages and farms would soon be under hundreds of feet of water. There was deep concern over the preservation of as much of their culture as possible — especially the dances — for (like all West African traditional dances) these were encapsulations of traditional thought, belief and history.[4] Archæologists attempted to find and save as much as they could in the areas to be inundated, and Father Steemers enlisted my help in his and the Society's efforts to save the most important dances.

In fact, it was Father Steemers who saved me from a potentially embarrassing situation concerning my contract with the University. I still had a year to go, when he suggested that instead of coming back to the University from Winneba (where I had become extremely unpopular owing to my attitudes toward traditional dancing even though I didn't insist upon teaching any of it), I might usefully spend the time between September 1969 and August 1970 editing two publications for the S.M.A.: one, a monthly magazine (*New Era*) for high school students; the second, a quasi-intellectual journal published biannually (*Insight and Opinion*). The priest responsible for these publications was rapidly approaching a nervous breakdown, and

---

4 See 1993. The Sokodae: A West African Dance. IN *Cultural Research Papers on Regional Cultures and Culture-Mixing.* (Ed. Tahir Shah), London: The Institute for Cultural Research and Octagon Press.

the S.M.A. wanted someone to keep the publications going while at the same time preparing for a Ghanaian take-over of both. The S.M.A. was willing to take over my contract and pay the University for housing on the campus and so the matter was settled.

Father Steemers planned to visit Holland for his annual leave in July 1969, and I wanted to visit England the end of June that year, as I had no holiday since my arrival in Ghana in 1967. Since I'd been invited to teach three orientation sessions for the British equivalent of the Peace Corps in Birmingham the last week in June, I decided to leave for England June twelfth so that I could spend at least a week in London before going to Birmingham. From there, I could travel to Holland, where I would meet Father Steemers in Oosterbeek (headquarters of the S.M.A.), so that arrangements for my new job in Accra could be made.

While in London, I visited the Royal Anthropological Institute Library on Threadneedle Street looking (as always) for publications about dancing. I was given several items, one of them by an author I'd never heard of: E.E. Evans-Pritchard. It was an essay written in 1928 on Azande dancing. I was so impressed with it I asked the librarian about the author, since the article was written the year I was born. For all I knew, the writer could be dead.

The librarian looked at me as if I had three heads and purple spots, saying with heavy emphasis that *Professor* Evans-Pritchard was head of the Institute of Social Anthropology at Oxford. The title didn't mean much to me, of course, because everybody who teaches in a university or college is called 'Professor' in the United States. I asked for his address, writing a letter that same day telling him how much I liked what he'd written. My letter finished, however, with the comment, "This is one of the best articles I have read on dancing, in spite of the fact you're not a dancer." Enclosing the letter in a large envelope with two of the published articles I'd written (The Dance of the Bedu Moon and Sokodae: Come and Dance). I posted the envelope and forgot about it.

Two days later, I received a note inviting me to come to Oxford, but our schedules didn't mesh. I had to leave for Birmingham on the day he suggested. In the interim he planned to go bird-watching in Devon. I sent a note thanking him, saying that I would write more from Ghana. I had no idea then that what I had written to him was to gain my entrance into Oxford, but more of that later.

Birmingham was fun, but relatively uneventful. It's amazing how self-conscious people are about their bodies. The best I could do was to tell the volunteers that if they would simply express their willingness to learn, the people they met in West Africa would be more than willing to teach them to dance. Apart from that I tried to emphasize the fact that dancing was much more than 'self-expression' and 'entertainment'.

My next stop was Holland, where I spent ten joyful and interesting days at the seminary in Oosterbeek, where I occupied the room reserved for visits by the Bishop. Father Steemers and I ate meals in a small dining room apart from the big refectory, but we met with all the priests after dinner in the common room, where I had my first taste of *Janvier* (a clear, fiery liquid drunk in one gulp after appropriate toasts had been made). I was also offered long, slim, mild Dutch cigars, which I grew to enjoy immensely.

I had several sessions with the priest who edited the magazines for which I was meant to assume responsibility. From him I learned about their formats and what I was expected to do with them upon my return. The rest of the time I spent in Holland was a holiday: Father Steemers and I traveled to Arnhem and nearby cities that played such an important part in World War II, as, indeed, he had, since he was a bicycle courier on several occasions for the Dutch underground while he was a seminary student. He had hair-raising tales to tell, in particular about carrying small consignments of supplies (radio tubes, and such) from one village to another hidden among sacks of potatoes or onions in his bicycle carrier.

I arrived back in Ghana in the middle of July rested, refreshed and brimming over with stories about my adventures, which a friend, Dr. Carleen O'Loughlin (nicknamed 'Paddy') wanted to hear. We were settled in on the verandah of her bungalow at the university with a gin and tonic apiece when I told her about my encounter at the R.A.I. (Royal Anthropological Institute) library. When I came to the part where the librarian revealed Evans-Pritchard's academic position, she interrupted me: "Do you have any idea who that man is?"

Realizing that I had committed some awful *gaffe*, I told her I didn't. She informed me that he was probably one of the most distinguished social anthropologists in England and that he was called 'Professor' because he was the head of the Institute. Only heads of departments and the like are referred to by that title in Britain. "Do you have a copy of the letter he wrote?" she asked. Handing the letter over, I wondered as she read it whether I'd have had the courage to write to him if I'd known who he was.

"You sent him one or two of the papers you've written?"

"I did, and he seemed interested in them," I said.

There was silence while we sipped our drinks, then Paddy leaned forward: "Drid, what are you going to do with the rest of your life? Have you ever thought of going back to university?"

"Sure, I've thought of that, but I won't. I've done all the interesting stuff, and at my age I won't go through sophomore gymnasium and all the other silly things they make you do to graduate."

"I don't mean go to university in the States" she said, "I mean go to Oxford or Cambridge."

Heartily laughing at such a ridiculous suggestion, I said, "You've got to be kidding. I'm too old. And remember, I didn't finish the undergraduate degree. I only spent three years and a bit at the University of Wisconsin."

Paddy was furious.

Chapter 14

> And that sweet City with her dreaming spires,
> She needs not June for beauty's heightening.
>
> (*Thrysis*, 1.19, Matthew Arnold)

Paddy got up from her chair leaning on her cane; she'd had polio when she was a young girl, leaving her right leg permanently disabled. She stumped around my chair only to vanish into the house where she checked on the progress of dinner, regaining her composure. She was a gallant lady: short and slightly heavy, a graduate in Economics from Cambridge and completely outspoken. She left her permanent home in Antigua for two years to come to Ghana where she did a feasibility study on the rum trade. She never married because "I couldn't find a man who's smarter than I am."

During her short absence, I thought, "Surely she's joking, but I'd better listen — find out what she's on about."

Paddy returned with a forty-page paper I'd tried to write on Krachi [KRAW-chee] dances, leaving it with her before I left for England. "What will you do with this kind of thing?" she demanded, waving the papers under my nose. "Wouldn't you like to find out whether you're talking nonsense or not?"

"It doesn't matter that you haven't finished a Bachelor's degree" she continued. "If someone at Oxford or Cambridge thinks you're intelligent enough, it doesn't matter whether you have a degree or whether you've been to school at all. It's clear Evans-Pritchard was impressed or he wouldn't have asked you to come to Oxford to meet him. What are you going to do about that? Have you written to him yet?" She plumped herself down into her chair.

"Have another drink. We must talk about this, but everything depends upon what you're going to do with your life."

"That's a damned difficult question, Paddy" I hedged. "Sure, I'd love to go to university in England but how could I manage? I don't know what social anthropology is and I haven't taken an exam for years."

"Face it" she retorted. "You only have a job here in Ghana for another year and what are you going to do after that? Opoku hates you so that puts paid to any further teaching at the University of Ghana. You didn't like Winneba because you don't want to teach ballroom dancing. You burned your bridges with the University of Wisconsin Extension when you turned down their offer to come back after Christmas last year and teach some balderdash about race relations. Looks to me like you've come to the end of the line — unless you've something else in mind." She took a long pull at her drink, peering at me over the rim of the glass.

"I don't" I said, looking into my empty glass wishing it were a crystal ball.

"That's not good enough" she snapped. "You've saved a little money, haven't you? Why couldn't those American friends — the Emeritus professors from Pennsylvania — help you?"

"I couldn't ask for help until I knew I could go" I retorted, getting up and moving to the drinks trolley where I replenished the gin and tonic. "Beside that, maybe I'm not good enough."

"Well, you'll never know unless you try. Why don't you let me help you write a letter to Evans-Pritchard? We'll send the letter along with this paper and see what he says."

"All right," I doubtfully agreed, but in the end, that is what we did. It took several weeks before the letter and the paper were ready to send. They were mailed in September 1969. By that time, I was wholly immersed in my new job, working with Father McAndrews and Brother Han from an office at the Accra Catholic Press downtown. Addy again took up residence in my house, but I no longer participated in his activities concerning the Institute or *Adzido*. I worked on the publications, talked with Father Steemers about the research trips we'd made and read books about social anthropology. I continued working on the book research project I had going about the Bedu masks

I'd collected in Nafana country. I became interested in masks and masked dancing in general, wanting to know more about other West African traditions that were in close proximity with the Bedus.

I originally learned of the masked dances of the Nafana people from Roy Seiber, an art historian who lived in Africa from time to time when he was commissioned for buying trips to Ghana, Ivory Coast, Nigeria and the Cameroon for various American museums. I had arranged for two sets of Bedu masks to be carved for me (one from the village of Tambi and the other from Sorobongo across the eastern Ghana border in the Ivory Coast), and it was now time to collect them.

The Bedu masks danced during the annual Muslim fast of Ramadan, which in 1969 took place during December. Addy and I planned to take the long trip to Nafana country over a period of three weeks for we had to collect not only masks, but drums and raffia body-coverings. It was a grueling trip through the heat, which seemed more intense than usual that year. The university's van, loaned for the duration of the trip, soon became covered with red dust, and it stayed that way until we returned to Accra.

No matter what time of year it was, travel was punctuated by four obligatory stops for Addy's prayers: at dawn, around noon, mid-afternoon and then in the evening. I shall always remember him unrolling, then placing his small rug (which he jokingly called 'my mosque') so that it faced Mecca, after which he washed his feet, hands and face. He would then stand at the edge of the rug, as he entered into his beloved ritual. The fact that he could neither eat nor drink between dawn and sunset during Ramadan made his observances special. When I asked him how he managed throughout the day, he said simply, "The prayers. Allah sustains me."

We traveled north to Kumasi, then east through Brong-Ahafo country to villages situated a few miles into Ivory Coast. We couldn't drive into Sorobongo. About three-quarters of a mile south of the village, the bush road ended. It became a footpath which meant that the masks and drums were carried to the van out of Sorobongo on our heads. We had almost enough people to accomplish this task by ourselves because on this trip I had a cook, two of Addy's brothers and a friend of his, Samuel Nortey, along. They had to learn the drumming and dancing of the Bedu masks as well as a men's dance, the *Gbain*.[1]

I heard a great deal about the *Gbain* dance, but never saw it in the bush. While in Tambi, I observed the general taboo on it for all women, staying in my hut after I heard the runner go through the village ringing a handbell warning women to stay inside and out of sight of the mask. I didn't believe that seeing the mask would make me barren or visit other possible ill-effects, but I preferred to conform to village beliefs about it, learning everything I could about the dance from Addy after I returned to Accra.

The Gbain shrine was situated out in the bush about a mile and a half east of Tambi. The men would congregate there and the observances would begin. The Nafana believe that there is an inherited, renegade force that resides in all males, which, if it isn't placated every six to eight weeks, will bring harm to the village and all its occupants. The shrine is tended by a 'mask-keeper' who generally wears the mask on the occasions when it dances.

There are several styles of Gbain mask; some are carved in the form of a crocodile maw or a buffalo's head, or (in the case of the one we brought back to Accra), the head of a wild bush-cow. Often, Gbain masks are helmet-style masks and many are fire-breathing masks, creating a fearsome spectacle in the dead of night as they leap, grunt, bellow and 'run wild' in the dance. The site of this dance is on the path from the shrine to and from the village and in the village itself. I heard Gbain singing and drumming. I heard the mask snort, paw and pant outside my hut, but didn't actually see it — nor did I want to in that context.

The Bedus were a different story. They represented benevolent male and female spirits that visited every compound

---

[1] See Williams, Drid. 1968. The Dance of the Bedu Moon. *African arts/arts d'Afrique*, Vol. 2, No. 2, University of California, Los Angeles. It is almost impossible to render the word, *gbain* into English, but [BAA] (as in 'Baa, Baa, Black Sheep') is close, provided 'Baa' isn't pronounced as the English do.

in the village during the Bedu moon. Two or three times a week during the Bedu moon, a dance was held which everyone attended and the Bedu masks would appear during these times. These masks made it possible for everyone in the village to start the new year's cycle with a clean slate, for they banished all the accumulated evil (in the form of sicknesses, crop failures, etc.) of the past year.

They also provided foils for groups of women (who would challenge the male mask) and groups of men (challenging the female mask) to rid themselves of all the real or imagined personal complaints they might have against the opposite sex which had happened during the year. These incidents were reviewed in the dance with (sometimes ribald) singing and explicit, suggestive gestures.

Except for the month of the Bedu moon, these masks "slept" — that is, they lay face-down, covered, over the rafters of a small hut built especially for them. The women who tended them entered now and again to renew their paint and to see if they were all right. After three or four years of serving the village in the manner in which they did, these masks were broken up and buried with ceremonies similar to that of people and a new pair would be carved. This is why so few Bedu masks exist outside of West Africa today. They are short-lived, and in fact, unless you came to a Nafana village during the last month of the lunar year (the Bedu moon), you would never know they existed. Frequently, the men who carve the masks are a special breed, who (like *Djeraba* [JER-ee-bah] who carved mine) was crippled from the waist down.

The trip back to Accra was slower than the trip out had been because the van was heavily loaded. We made a long stop at the Ghana/Ivory Coast border, too, while papers concerning the masks were checked to see that I was not leaving with any national treasures. We spent Christmas eve in Brong-Ahafo country at the home of a student of Roy Seiber's who had saved a bottle of brandy for the holiday. He was studying art history with Roy, engaged in field research for a Doctoral degree. I made a poor showing as a guest that night for, after drinking some of the brandy and eating a couple of skewers of flame-broiled pieces of grass-cutter,[2] I fell asleep! I vaguely remember Addy helping me stumble into the house to a bed, where I slept fully-clothed and uninterrupted until noon Christmas day.

To say I was 'tired' is an understatement: wrestling a loaded van over bush roads in the heat of the sun is no joke, but the trip to Tambi and Sorobongo was memorable for other reasons. It was the last research trip I made in West Africa and I came back with two pairs of Bedu masks and their accessories. The accessories included musical instruments, all of which would reside in the Liverpool Museum, along with slides, etc. during the first eighteen months of my stay in Oxford. Actually, the Tambi masks traveled with me to the United States and subsequently, to Australia, but the Sorobongo masks had to be sacrificed in 1971. I sold them to a collector — a jazz musician — in London to help pay for my B.Litt. thesis. I still have the Tambi masks which, between 1990 and 1994 were enjoyed by people all over Australia in an international exhibition called 'Ritual' sponsored by the Australian Museum.

As much as I loved traveling in Ghana and the Ivory Coast, I realized by this time that what I didn't know about doing field research into dances would fill several books. I was eager to hear from Evans-Pritchard, because thoughts of the possibility of going to university began to push everything else aside. Finally, in late January, I received an Airletter with an official letterhead which contained three sentences: "Dear Miss Williams" it said, "I will retire as Professor of the Institute of Social Anthropology in June this year (1970). However, I think you should come to Oxford and take a Diploma and B.Litt. in social anthropology. Please write to the Diploma Secretary, Mr. Edwin Ardener. Yours sincerely, Professor E.E. Evans-Pritchard."

Paddy and I celebrated that night in high style, but, receiving Evans-Pritchard's letter was only a beginning. I wrote to Mr. Ardener straightaway, to be answered with a packet of forms that had to be filled out, etc. After sending those away, everything dropped into a well of silence. By the middle of May,

---

2 A fairly large animal, weighing from five to fifteen pounds; member of the rat family, who eats savanna grass and seeds and is considered a delicacy by local people.

I had still received no word from Oxford, and Paddy was getting fed up. She decided that I should go to her university — Cambridge — working things out so that I spent a day with Dr. Jack Goody (in Ghana because he was an external examiner for the sociology/social anthropology department at the University) telling him about the masks and the dances I'd studied. The upshot of this was that I was enrolled in Cambridge, assigned to Lucy Cavendish House, before I received an answer from Oxford late in June.

I'm not sure Paddy ever really forgave me, but when I was accepted at St. Hugh's College in Oxford and told them I could start in Michaelmas Term, 1970, the die was cast. I chose Oxford over Cambridge because I preferred the writings of Oxford anthropologists over those at Cambridge — Evans-Pritchard, Lienhardt, Beattie, Ardener, Needham, Riviere — it was a great faculty, as I soon discovered when I had to write papers for them starting in October that year.

Uprooting myself from living for three and a half years in West Africa wasn't an easy task. It was complicated in my case by completing the responsibilities I had to the S.M.A. and the Accra Catholic Press, including handing everything over to the new Ghanaian editor. Somehow, it all got done. I learned many things in Ghana, but three items will always stand out: 1. the ancient British art of 'muddling through'; 2. the West African art of engaging all your friends to help with any major undertaking and 3. the time-honored custom of bargaining. Roy Seiber introduced me to the latter as a participant. Before meeting him, I'd been nothing but an observer. Watching him expertly deal with Hausa traders over sculptures, beads, and other artifacts made me want to learn, because there is much more to bargaining than a mere business transaction.

An object isn't merely an object, for a start. It is an emblem of a social relationship. There is the person who made (carved, molded, whittled or cast) the object and there is the person (or persons) who originally owned the object. There is the Hausa trader who has acquired the object and there is the person who now wants to be the owner. Uppermost in everyone's mind (and crucial to the outcome of the transaction) is how much the buyer and trader know.

For example, the first time I saw Roy Seiber in action, he was interested in Ashanti gold weights — delightful little carved metal figures made to put on one side of a balance to determine the price, in ounces, of gold. They had been used for many years in Ghana. Roy's knowledge of these was crucial because, owing to the high demand for the little figures, a fraudulent trade had started. Small figures were 'aged' quite simply by digging a hole in the ground, putting newly-fashioned figures in the hole, adding lavish amounts of urine, potash and other substances to the figures and leaving them buried for a few months, after which time, they appeared to be 'old'. To the untrained eye, the bogus gold weights looked as if time had created their *patina*, which wasn't true, of course. Wood could be aged in similar ways, and made to look as if it had been used, perhaps assaulted by termites, etc. A stool that might look very old and which the trader said belonged to an ancestral shrine may really only have existed for a few months. Both parties in the transaction knew these things, but neither referred directly to any of it. Bargaining was an informal ritual.

Traders would approach Roy's house, announce their presence to the cook-steward, then wait until Roy appeared, announcing that he was open to viewing the trader's wares. At this time, the trader would transfer a large bundle from his shoulder to the floor of the verandah, spread the cloths that held the bundle together and arrange what he had on the cloth. Sitting cross-legged on one edge of the cloth or on a small carpet he waited. Roy sat opposite. Greetings were exchanged, coffee, tea or mineral water was brought to them and they drank together, inquiring into the health and well-being of their respective families.

After these preliminaries, the trader delicately mentioned something about the "poor miserable things he brought" saying he was forced to sell what he had in order to support his wives and children who were (invariably) close to starvation somewhere in Nigeria. Moreover, he was sure he had nothing that would really interest such an important scholar (Roy had a reputation among the traders!), except for one or two sculptures that were so rare and precious he really didn't want to sell them. He hadn't put them on display because he hoped Roy would be generous, choosing something that *was* on display to help him out.

Tobacco in some form was brought, and the trader's opening gambit was contemplated in silence by both men (and anyone else who happened to be present) while more drinks were brought. Wisps and curls of smoke added their fragrance to that of the masses of flowers that surrounded the house. Thin strips of sunlight penetrated the bamboo blinds' shade, creating a hazy, dappled light.

Roy's hand moved toward a pile of carved wooden hair combs near where he sat on the edge of the floor-cloth. He said nothing, but picked up a huge comb decorated with an attached circle of lovely small beads. He examined the comb, turning it over and over. "Comb for goddess?" he asked.

"Comb for Kpele [PAY-lay]" was the answer, "bought from Accra-man whose wife, a priestess, died."

"Hmm" Roy mused, putting the large comb down and picking up two smaller, battered ones."How much for these?"

At least an hour went by before price was mentioned and then only in relation to relatively unimportant objects.

Roy always bought something, but he was really interested in the objects the trader had *not* displayed. A trading session could last as much as four hours. The average time was between two and a half and three. The nature of the potential transaction and the price of the important objects the trader brought determined the elements of interchange and the length of time required to negotiate. The nitty-gritty was eventually reached after the trader stated an absurdly high price which Roy countered with an equally absurd price that was far too low. Finally, they settled on a price in between and nobody lost face. Mutual enjoyment and satisfaction was reached through the shrewd verbal manipulations that occurred during the process.

Not all bargaining in West Africa took this much time, of course. Taking a taxi from Accra to the university or buying a dozen eggs in the market only required two or three minutes, but unless one was a complete newcomer, no price was accepted the first time 'round. Larger transactions such as those I had to make for a truck and driver to take my belongings to the ship's pier in Tema took approximately half an hour — long enough to consume a bottle of mineral water or a cup of tea — but no matter what was involved, price had to be negotiated. Would the driver bring his mates to load and unload the crates, or would I supply this kind of labor? Would I want to ride in the truck with the driver or would I have my own vehicle? There were several details requiring mutually agreeable decisions.

In the end, Addy and his brothers supplied the labor and some of them rode on the truck with my belongings, while some rode in the Volvo with me. We lived with packing cases, cleaned the local carpenter's shops out of baskets of wood-shavings (the best material for packing) and, in the end, I left Ghana with two steamer trunks, two large suitcases and eight hundred cubic feet of drums, masks, gongs, raffias and other paraphernalia which would be required when (and if) Addy was able to come to England. Addy and his family fell heir to the Volvo and all the belongings I had that couldn't be taken to England with me.

I subsequently traveled from Tema to Liverpool on the *HMS Aureole*. In fact, it was her final voyage before she was scrapped, as she was the last of a fleet of ships that had transferred English colonists and troops from England to West Africa for many years. English influence was by that time rapidly waning in Ghana. The day I arrived in 1967 was the first anniversary of the *coup d'etat* of the National Liberation Council [NLC], the military *junta* that overthrew Kwami Nkrumah. The NLC represented the second of several difficult steps towards full-scale self-rule and independence.

It was hard to leave the many friends I'd made in Ghana — especially Paddy, whom I never saw again. Although I heard from her the first two years I was in Oxford, she fell ill and died early in 1973 after she returned to Antigua in 1972. I had hoped to see her again, as the last letter I had from her outlined plans to visit England for Christmas that year. Her death brought much heartache , not only because I lost one of the best friends I ever had, but because Evans-Pritchard also died in 1973. A pattern emerged in relation to my life.

I saw how much all my relationships had been influenced over the years because I was afraid of saying good-bye to anyone I knew because I might never see them again. I'd casually said 'See you later' to my mother and never saw her again. I'd said good-bye to Daddy — and didn't see him again until after he was in prison. He died while I was in England. I thought I'd see both grandmothers again, but didn't because they died unexpectedly while I was many miles away. The last relative I lost in this way was Auntie Margaret who died suddenly and grievously in Portland, Oregon in 1966.

I realized that no matter what I had to do or say, I invariably found myself placating people, telling little white lies about how I felt, compromising myself in many ways. I constantly 'smoothed things over' because I couldn't bear to part with anyone if there were bad feelings between us. I didn't fully comprehend until Paddy died how much I'd suffered in subtle ways because I couldn't put the fears I felt about losing people behind me once and for all. I thought of Rilke's wise observation: "Thus we live, forever taking leave" (1923 -*Duino Elegies, VIII*).

During the long, leisurely voyage of the *Aureole* up the African coast to the Canary Islands, northward over the Atlantic past Europe to Liverpool and England, I concentrated less on taking leave of West Africa and thought more about the many meetings still to come. How would I get on at Oxford? *Would* I 'get on' or was I past that? Paddy was convinced that age made no difference.

"It's worrying about it that will defeat you if you let it" she said, "Think about other things." And I did. Thanks to her, I had a room to go to at an address that still makes me smile: 111 Divinity Road. It was also thanks to Paddy that a representative from the Liverpool Museum waited for me when the ship docked. She believed (and she was right) that the Museum would want to display the masks and other artifacts I had with me. She told me how to arrange for bed and breakfast for two nights in Liverpool while I made arrangements with the Museum, how to store my trunks temporarily in 'Left Luggage' and how to book tickets on a train to Oxford when I could go there unencumbered. She explained the structure of Oxford University and talked about the poet/critic, Matthew Arnold (1822-1888) and his "dreaming spires."

She told me about St. Hugh's College, whose Principal was famous owing to the archæological excavations she carried out in Jerusalem and Jericho. I never knew for sure, but always believed that Paddy wrote to her, for the welcome I received from Kathleen Kenyon was everything I could have hoped for and more. After two days in Liverpool, I collected my luggage and boarded the train for Oxford. I could scarcely believe my good fortune! I arrived at Oxford station midday, bundled everything into a taxi and headed for Divinity Road. I didn't even unpack my things immediately. I was eager to visit the center of the town.

About two o'clock, I got off the double-decker bus at Cornmarket (the central square of the town where the High Street and Cornmarket Street meet). I stood facing 'The High' knowing that Christ Church College was a few blocks to my right on St. Aldate's, the Examination Schools and St. Mary's were in front of me, and the Institute of Social Anthropology was about a mile past St. Michael's Street, George Street and St. Giles up the Banbury Road to my left. I stood there in the August sunlight savoring a strange feeling that came over me: I was 'home.' I'd finally made it!

Psychologists say that *déjà vu* is "an illusory feeling of having already experienced a present situation" — and so much for what psychologists think. How do they know whether such feelings are "illusory" or not? There is a knowing coincident with 'be-ing' that is ineluctable. I'd been in England before and in and around London several times. No such thoughts occurred to me there, nor have they in any other place I've been in the world. There was never anything *tediously* familiar about Oxford, or the experiences I had during the time I lived there. Every time I went away from and came back to Oxford, I had the same feeling of coming home. In fact, I've never felt really at home in any other place throughout my adult life.

For the next three weeks, I became acquainted with the city. I visited the Bodleian and Ashmolean libraries, toured several colleges (New College was my favorite), rode buses all over the city, walked in Port Meadow. I met June Anderson, the librarian for the Institute, who, together with Barbara Allaway, the administrative assistant to Professor Maurice Friedman, turned out to be special friends.

Barbara and June helped smooth what might otherwise have been a rocky path for me because they generously shared the wealth of information they had about the faculty and what was expected of new Diploma students.

Chapter 15

> Very nice sort of place, Oxford, I should think,
> for people who like that sort of place.
>
> (G. B. Shaw, *Man and Superman*, Act II).

My first encounter with Edwin Ardener (the man who later became my Doctoral supervisor) was interesting because, to my mind, it proved the depth and extent of a stigma I carried — that of being so closely associated with dancing.

"The faculty" he said, "thinks it might be better for you — that you would be more successful — if you did a Diploma[1] in ethnology rather than social anthropology. They wonder how you might feel about that?"

"I don't feel anything" I replied, "because I have no idea what either subject amounts to. What's the difference between the two qualifications?"

He explained that in the British system at that time, ethnology was mainly connected with museums, the collection of artifacts and the essentially descriptive kinds of writing that were associated with these. He said the faculty imagined that, as dances (especially in Africa), were excellent representatives of "material culture" (i.e. masks, musical instruments, special costuming, etc.), ethnology was probably the field in which I would be most productive. Perhaps dances were linked more closely to folk lore than they were to anthropology.

---

1 If one were admitted as a graduate student in social anthropology at Oxford, the completion of a year's course called a 'Diploma' was required regardless of previous university affiliation or how many degrees one might have. One member of my class had a Ph.D. from a German university, and other foreign students had Master's degrees, but none of that mattered. The Diploma was a proving ground from which one was either encouraged to continue or given terminal certification for the year's work.

I tried drawing him out further: "The faculty doesn't think I could cope with the Diploma in social anthropology, then?" I asked.

He said they hadn't made any final judgment, adding that social anthropology was, in a word, much more theoretical than ethnology. Since I had demonstrated strong interests in the dances themselves and their paraphernalia, they were simply trying to help me make the best choice. The faculty's deductions about the focus of my interest was reasonable based on what they knew of me, but they wanted to know what I thought.

"I'm afraid I can't be of much help because I don't know how well I will manage going back to school after several years, but I'd like to try social anthropology. If I can't make the grade, I'll shift to ethnology. Could I do that?"

"You can't say fairer than that" he replied, smiling slightly, telling me to appear at the Institute in a week's time (October seventh at eleven a.m.) for an orientation session where I would meet my Diploma supervisor and other members of the faculty. Michaelmas term lectures would commence the following day.

Thanks to June Anderson, I already knew who my Diploma supervisor was: Godfrey Lienhardt. I was somewhat awed by him, as I had read two of his books[2] and at the time, I couldn't imagine what his relationship to graduate students might be. I had seen Evans-Pritchard once, but only from a distance. He had a room on the third floor of the Institute — an old Victorian building that housed offices, lecture-rooms, library and all. June was a gold mine of information about everyone. It was she who introduced me to Barbara Allaway who, I was told, really "ran" everything, because she kept records, knew where things were and had been at the Institute from the beginning of Evans-Pritchard's tenure.

The Institute's common room was in the basement. I arrived early, walking from St. Giles because it was a lovely mild

---

2 Lienhardt, G. 1961. *Divinity and Experience*. London: Oxford University Press, which is about Dinka religion, and *Social Anthropology*, 1966 (also Oxford University Press).

autumn day. "Life really does begin at forty" I thought to myself as I sauntered along, "only you're a bit late, Drid — in five days, you'll be forty-two — but who cares? What an adventure! Pity you won't have grandchildren to share it with, but there'll be plenty of students in future who will be interested." My heart sang. Words can't describe how happy I was to be there. Barbara and June officiated at the tea-urn outside the common room. Collecting a cup of strong tea and a cookie (which I already called 'biscuit') I joined my fellow-students who were arranged around the periphery of the common room, displaying varying degrees of discomfort.

Among them were Carol, an African-American student who had taken a Master's degree in sociology at a Canadian university; Kwami, a graduate from University of Ghana seeking a B.Litt. degree; Robert, a Jesuit priest from Belgium whose degrees were from Louvain; Ahmed from Libya and an assortment of British students (including the grandson of the famous economist, John Maynard Keynes) who had completed their undergraduate work. All told, we numbered twenty-two, of which five were women.[3]

I found a place to stand next to the bronze bust of Evans-Pritchard displayed on a stand at one side of a huge bay window which had a view of the Banbury Road outside. Just as I was about to replenish my cup of tea, an old man entered the room. He wore faded olive-green corduroy trousers decorated with a few stains here and there, matching the somewhat threadbare old cardigan that didn't fully cover a shirt which had seen better days. His hands were clasped behind his back. A hush fell. His head, with its imposing shock of white hair and bristling eyebrows was thrust forward. He advanced counter-clockwise around the room, greeting each of us, followed by a disreputable-looking roly-poly dog that (until it died later that year) followed him everywhere.

When he reached me, he stopped and said, "So you're the dancer?"

---

[3] Of the students in the '70-'71 Diploma class, thirteen were encouraged to continue on to the B.Litt. and of this group, only two — Nigel Barley and I — eventually finished with Doctoral degrees.

"I am" I admitted, wondering what would come next.

"Well ... hmm (there was a pause as he looked me up and down), do you think you can write a thesis that anthropologists who aren't dancers can understand?"

Blushing, never dreaming that he'd remember what I'd written at the end of my first letter to him, I grinned sheepishly.

"I don't know but I'll surely try!"

"Good!" He smiled, shook my hand, and said, "Come and see me in six months' time."

Escaping to the tea-urn, I told Barbara and June what he'd said. Before they could reply, Godfrey Lienhardt appeared.

"It seems that you are one of my tutorial students. After you've had tea, come to my room upstairs with the other four and get your first assignment."

Godfrey's tutorial students that year were the Jesuit priest, the Ghanaian, the African-American girl, the German bloke who had a Doctoral degree — and me. We were a motley crew, but willing enough, although I shouldn't speak for the others. 'Willingness' was about all I had, really, because I certainly didn't have any of the advanced education they represented. Nevertheless, I was there, and that fact alone counted for something!

Our encounter with Dr. Lienhardt was brief. After greeting and welcoming us to the Institute, he said, "I want to set the question for your first essay. Do you have paper? You'd better write it down. The question is this: *In how far does ecology explain the social structure of the Nuer and in how far does it not*? You will each come to this office on Tuesday of next week for your first tutorial. You may go now unless you have questions."

Needless to say, I had questions — lots of them — but none I felt I could ask him! I escaped to the library where I sat looking at the small notebook in which the question was written. The only thing I knew about 'ecology' was what I'd learned from a book I'd read by Rachel Carson, *The Silent Spring*. I had no idea where — or how 'the Nuer' lived, far less who they were. As for what Dr. Lienhardt meant by 'social structure', I hadn't a clue. As I sat meditating on the depth of my ignorance, another graduate student to whom I'd spoken once or twice came into the library — Malcolm Crick.

"What's the matter, Drid?" he asked. "You look a bit forlorn."

"I'm supposed to write an essay for next week and I don't know where to begin."

"Maybe I can help. What's the question?" (Malcolm was writing his D.Phil. thesis, and although he was seventeen years younger than I, we became very good friends). I showed him the question.

"Oh, that's a simple one" he said. "Godfrey's being easy on you."

"My God!" I exploded, "If this is *easy*, I hate to think what hard questions might be like!"

"Never mind" he said soothingly, "You'll get the hang of it in a few weeks. First, get hold of E.P.'s book, *The Nuer*. There's a long section on ecology in it. Just make sure you read the whole book and that you understand what E.P.'s on about. You might look up 'social structure' in the *International Encyclopædia of the Social Sciences*. That's usually helpful for Diploma students — and one more thing: whatever else you do in your paper, *make sure you answer the question*. If you don't, Godfrey will tear you to shreds."

"Thanks, Malcolm. I owe you. How about dinner tomorrow night?"

"Some other time. I have a seminar from seven to ten on Wednesdays. See you in Ardener's lecture in the morning. Cheerio and good luck." He left.

By this time, June was back behind her desk, so I checked out a copy of *The Nuer* and headed for the *Gardener's Arms* pub where I ate a shepherd's pie while I read.

Time flew. A week later, I stood nervously outside Godfrey's rooms at four p.m. clutching my paper which was thirteen foolscap ('legal size') pages long, including five pages of notes. I knocked, not knowing what to expect.

"Come in — and do sit down" he said, turning towards me in his swivel chair, then turning back to the old-fashioned roll-top desk to pick up his pipe and tobacco pouch.

After I'd seated myself on the sofa across from his desk on the other side of a bay window with a peaceful view of treetops, towers and late afternoon sunshine, he turned towards me again.

"What have you there?"

"My paper" I replied, holding it out toward him.

"How long is it?" he asked, pushing the tobacco firmly into the pipe.

"Thirteen pages with five pages of notes" I said faintly, my answer causing him to swivel back to the desk, then on around three hundred sixty degrees to face me again. The beautiful Cambridge accent was precise:

"You may read five pages to me. *Any* five pages will do, but *only* five pages." He drew deeply on his pipe, looked at the ceiling and blew smoke rings.

I did the fastest précis I'd ever done in my life, reading some bits from the beginning, the middle and the end of the essay, making sure I concluded by answering his question. There was silence while we watched the fragrant pipe smoke curl gently upwards through a stray shaft of sunlight.

"That's not too bad" he said. "In future, you need only write five, possibly six, pages. Americans tend to write too much. If you have nothing to say, five pages is quite enough to say it — sheer volume of words won't make a difference. If you have something to say, the gist is easily captured in five pages. Your question for next week is this: What does Mary Douglas's *Purity and Danger* add to Franz Steiner's concept of taboo? You may go now. Thank you. I'll see you again next week."

Dizzy with relief and filled with pride that I seemed to have got something right, I was glad to find Malcolm again in the library where I went to check out Douglas's book and Steiner's *Taboo*.

"How did it go?" Malcolm asked.

"Let's go have a pint and some supper and I'll tell you all about it."

Three hours later, I was satisfied that most of my perceptions about the essay session were true. Socratic method was used in teaching and yes, by the end of the Diploma year, I would write twenty-four essays — one per week — but not all for Godfrey. It was necessary to get used to different styles of questions and the individuals who went along with them. Yes, the Diploma exams were all essay questions, and the best thing I'd ever done in the undergraduate study I'd had in Wisconsin was to learn to write a good précis.

No, I wasn't stupid because I didn't understand anything Ardener said in his lectures. In Malcolm's opinion (and later in mine) Ardener was the most erudite member of faculty. What I needed to do was to take notes on what I didn't understand and then make it my business to find out what he was on about. That trail was to lead me to Chomsky, Saussure, communication theory and the whole world of linguistic anthropology about which I knew nothing. Oxford was my 'Open Sesame' to many worlds and, from the beginning, I decided to learn — to absorb all I could. It was all up to me. That's what made it so different from the previous university experience I'd had.

At Oxford, no one made students go to lectures. If someone could get through the Diploma without attending lectures, well and good. No one took attendance, required medical excuses for absences and such. There were no 'course outlines'. Book lists were available, but what was the point? One discovered the requirements through other means — mainly the tutorial sessions. Politics didn't enter into the learning process the way I'd remembered at Wisconsin and that point was brought home to me through a comment John Beattie made during a tutorial session on kinship. Naturally, I'd read his book, *Other Cultures*, and discovered that, theoretically, he was a functionalist. The approach that appealed to me, however, was structuralist. Halfway through my paper, he interrupted:

"Tell me, Miss Williams, do you think functional approaches to kinship are a load of old rubbish?"

I squeaked out, "Yes, although I can see why some find a functionalist approach more satisfying."

"Good" he said, smiling, "Now we can get on with it. I trust you can defend your position."

And that was the whole point. No more 'pussy-footing'. No more having to agree with lecturers, even if you didn't, for fear of getting bad grades. No more arguments that were ill-disguised quarrels over hurt feelings. You weren't expected to 'agree' with anything. The only requirement was to produce a good, well-argued case.

I reflected on such things wandering through the gardens and cloistered walks at New College (built in 1290). I thought about the sources of knowledge while examining the portraits of John Locke, Lewis Carroll and others hanging on the walls of the refectory at Christ Church. It was there that I finally got rid of the awe I felt for professors and celebrated thinkers.

"They've all sat at these tables, struggled with examinations, got caught out by the proctors for returning late to college" I said to myself.

"They've struggled with questions that many times turned out to be imponderables, just as I do."

Staring up at Locke's picture I thought, "I don't believe you were right about people being *tabula rasas* and it's perfectly all right for me to think and say so." Intellectually, my emancipation began at that moment and what a great feeling *that* was!

Meanwhile, back at the Institute, my education, formal and informal, continued. I discovered that Malcolm attended lectures in philosophy of science. Joining him one morning, I encountered a veritable Barishnikov of the lecture platform — Rom Harré — who, together with his colleague, Peter Secord, was writing *The Explanation of Social Behaviour*. I attended Harré's lectures the whole time I was at Oxford. In fact, he was the internal examiner for the D.Phil., but more of that later. I sometimes became so engrossed in Harré's platform-performance that I missed what he was saying. Nor did it escape my notice that his style was radically different from Ardener, who was so self-effacing he seemed to fade into the brickwork if you didn't listen very carefully.

In contrast to both of these was Lienhardt who began the first lecture he gave that year by extracting several of Sir James Frazer's letters from an old shoe-box tied with a bit of string, loaned from the Royal Anthropological Institute. He read passages from the letters. Ultimately, it was from Lienhardt that I learned what an academic discipline really is, no matter how muddled or perverted it may become through human error and carelessness. It is a prolonged intense struggle to discover some part of the truth about things.

I also learned that our predecessors' mistakes (and Sir James's inheritors still make many of these) are as important as their insights which stand the test of time. Anthropology was known as "Mr. Tylor's science" at Oxford in its earliest years for the good reason that E.B. Tylor traveled. His concept of anthropology was based on first-hand experience. Frazer's wasn't, although neither of them had much of lasting value to say about dancing.[4] And, it was about dancing that I first talked to Evans-Pritchard after six months passed when I visited him in March as he had directed.

I only spoke to him before that time during the week I was in the Radcliffe Hospital early in December. He turned up, a bouquet of flowers in hand, to find out how I had recovered from an hysterectomy, made necessary by the discovery of a large, benign uterine tumor which, unknown to me, had developed while I was in Ghana.

E.P. was curious about the operation: "Must be like having your balls cut off" he ventured, glancing at me sideways.

"No, not really" I told him, "because the fallopian tubes weren't removed; just the uterus." I finally had to draw a diagram.

It was interesting to be his informant because I found out what it was like to be on the receiving end of determined anthro-

---

4 See Chapter 4: Intellectualistic and Literary Explanations [of the dance] in Williams's *Ten Lectures on Theories of the Dance* (1991: 68-75. Full reference on p. 106-112).

pological questioning. He resolutely set about finding out what the operation entailed, mainly, I think, because he'd heard the doctors used *curare* (an exotic South American poison) during the procedure. I recovered rapidly and without complications in time to attend the final week of lectures before the Christmas holiday.

By this time, I'd moved from the Divinity Road address taking up residence in a graduate student house owned by St. Hugh's College. I remember this experience with mixed pleasure and mild exasperation, shared by seven of us over the problem created by an associate (an Indian girl from Madras) whose meticulous observance of Hindu purification rituals not only monopolized the upstairs bathroom at crucial times, but deprived us of hot water most of the time. It seemed a small price to pay for the convenience of living two blocks from the Institute, however, and nobody made formal complaints. On the whole, we were all too busy studying, attending seminars and preparing for examinations.

None of this was like the cramming for finals that I'd been accustomed to at Wisconsin. It was a far more serious process; mainly, I think, because of the general emphasis on language, and the high values placed on literacy in spoken and written forms throughout the University. By the time April came around, I suffered from severe eyestrain, the result of which was my first pair of eyeglasses. I only had to wear them while reading, but that was most of the time.

Godfrey's assistance proved invaluable as I prepared for what was to come. He was aware of my fears regarding the possibility of not passing the Diploma, so he suggested a strategy that worked very well: I did fifty exercises for him based upon questions in past exam papers. By the time I arrived at 'Schools' on the morning of June fourth, I felt I had a reasonable chance of getting through the twenty-one hours of writing (seven three-hour periods over four days) that were in store for us.

Chapter 16

> Reason is not come to repeat the universe but to fulfil it.
>
> (George Santayana, *Life of Reason*, vol.V, History, ch.ii)

A week before the exams, I had a vivid dream. The setting was a lovely garden where I hosted a large buffet dinner. All the guests at the party were anthropologists (and a few philosophers), many of whom I'd never seen, of course, because I only knew them as authors of books. In my dream they appeared as I imagined them even if I'd never seen them. It was a civilized party; well-dressed people exhibiting their best behavior who earnestly (often heatedly) talked to one another as they ate sitting at tables in groups of three or more. I didn't eat anything, but found myself going from one group to another making futile attempts to get them to agree with each other. I fruitlessly strove to reconcile irreconcilable differences. Only a few of my guests agreed about anything and I awoke thoroughly exhausted — exhausted and astonished. Was it really twenty-six years ago that the fear of disagreement of any kind had been instilled? Could I do something about it? I'd never fully understood important differences between quarelling (what my parents did) and argument (the universe of discourse in which I now participated). It was through insights like these that the pressure of the exams greatly increased my understanding of self and others.

I've heard that Diploma exams aren't the same now as they were in June 1971 when our class took them. Rumor has it that they are easier — which makes me thankful that I went through them when I did. Although the 'pass' I received wasn't particularly distinguished, their length and difficulty marked all degrees of passing as special. I got through — in itself an achievement. It was a unique experience. For me, the exams were a rite of passage into a new life.

We started on a Thursday with two sets of papers: 'History, Theory and Relation to Other Disciplines' from nine to twelve, and 'Kinship and Marriage Relations' from one to four. Friday was 'Law and Juridical Relations' in the morning and 'Economics and Ecology' in the afternoon. We had the weekend off. Monday was the area paper in the morning (I did the African option) and 'Witchcraft, Magic and Religion' in the afternoon. For all these papers, we were required to write answers to three out of twelve questions. Tuesday (the final day), we wrote for three hours in the morning on one question. Following the whole ordeal, the courtyard of 'Schools' was filled with students and well-wishers. Popping champagne corks punctuated an atmosphere charged with relief. There were hugs, kisses and high spirited banter: festivity was the order of the day.

A week later, I was told I could go on with a B.Litt. and I could choose my supervisor, which was Ardener, for both B.Litt. and D.Phil. A change of residence accompanied my change of scholarly status because inflation had started in England. Even though the Principal arranged for me to pay the same fees I paid upon arrival at St. Hughes, I had to make some money to survive. The problem was solved by the Russian Orthodox community who owned two graduate student houses (St. Macrina and St. Gregory houses) and a small church located near the Institute. They wanted someone to live rent-free in St. Macrina house in exchange for a thorough weekly cleaning of the entire house which was occupied by seven theological students. Not only was the room rent-free, I was given five pounds per week for my labor. Late in June 1971, I moved into the attic on the fourth floor of St. Macrina house, which was big enough to accommodate the drums, masks, etc. which were sent from the Liverpool Museum in July of that year.

It was in these circumstances that work on the B.Litt. degree commenced based on a decision — made with E.P.'s assistance — that it would be about social anthropology and the dance. I was excited by the prospect but dubious about his comment, "Regardless of how it turns out, it will be the first thesis written on the subject in this university for eight hundred years." I couldn't tolerate the thought that the thesis might be memorable only because it was the first of its kind. I wanted the B.Litt. to turn out well!

The survey of literature that comprises the first half of *Ten Lectures* (see pp. 1 through 150) was the initial task. I quickly found that writing a book-length document was not as easy as I'd anticipated. I wrote seventeen drafts of the first chapter for Mr. Ardener. For several weeks, I thought I'd never get past that chapter, but by the time I finished the whole thesis the first week in November 1972, I could handle the writing. I simply translated Johnson's remark, made in 1750: "A man may write at any time, if he will set himself doggedly to it." If men can write at any time by setting themselves doggedly to it, so can women.

Writing is a lot like dancing, if you want to be good at it, you practice every day. The occasional public performances are the result of continuous private rehearsal. I found that the disciplines I'd practiced for thirty years as a dancer didn't let me down. They worked as well in the medium of sound and written language as they did in movement and body language. Skillful results in either medium are comparable. Excellent writing, like exceptionally good dancing seems to observers to be effortless. "Spontaneous — natural," people say, but it is effortlessness and spontaneity that are the results of years of discipline and hard work. As Anna Pavolva often said during her lifetime, "You learn [ballet] technique so that you can forget it."[1]

One of the reasons I so enjoy teaching sociocultural anthropology to dancers, after leaving Oxford, is that many of them approach their studies in the same spirit. They bring the discipline and hard work associated with their dance forms along with them and, for a significant number of the students I've so far been privileged to teach, anthropology became what it was for me: an orgy of discovery about the life of the mind.

It didn't surprise me that the teaching methods used at the Institute were Socratic, nor did it surprise me to find some similarities in Evans-Pritchard's thought to that of Montaigne, who remarked, "Someone said to Socrates that a certain man

---

1 The vow I'd made when I was sixteen (p. 19) about "learning to talk really well" finally came true. I'd never be inarticulate about anything, ever again, and that included dancing.

had grown no better by his travels. 'I should think not,' he said, 'he took himself along with him.'" (I: 39, 76).[2] I'm not at all sure I grew by traveling to West Africa, because I took myself along with me, not having any other recourse. I'd had no prior education to assist me towards any other view.

Anthropology changed all that, because E.P. (somewhat like I imagined Socrates to think) sought for a middle-ground in social anthropology that avoided excesses of any kind. Although it was from David Pocock that I developed my individual application of the idea of a personal anthropology, it was from E.P. that I realized how wrong it is to judge everything in the light of one's own personal circumstances, imagining that what one sees and believes to be good in personal situations holds true for everyone else in the real world.

More than anything else, however, Oxford taught me to acknowledge the great achievements of human beings by honoring the foundation of the achievements in people themselves. Pocock's idea of a personal anthropology (like Polanyi's *Personal Knowledge* which inspired it) consistently emphasizes the importance of the *person* in the process of knowing.

Evans-Pritchard was convinced that social anthropology was a special kind of historiography. He regarded the subject as one of the humanities, not as a natural science. In his famous Marett Lecture (1950), he couldn't resist observing that "[A]s the history of anthropology shows, positivism leads very easily to a misguided ethics, anæmic scientific humanism or — Saint-Simon and Comte are cases in point — *ersatz* religion."[3]

He was contemptuous of those who wanted to diminish human societies to the status of natural systems "which can be reduced to variables" (1962: 28). He savagely criticized those who believe that human beings are nothing but stimulus-response mechanisms, cybernetic systems and biochemical organisms. He refused to let social anthropology be reduced to physics, chemistry and biology because he didn't believe that

---

2 Frame, Donald M. (Trans.). 1965. *The Complete Essays of Montaigne*, Stanford, Cal.: Stanford University Press.

3 *Essays in Social Anthropology*. London: Faber and Faber, 1962, p. 27.

human behavior was the result of conglomerations of atoms or that our knowledge of ourselves and others is only true when it approximates the standards of mechanistic scientific measurements.

I basked in the sunlight of these ideas, not because everyone at Oxford believed them — they didn't — but because at Oxford, I could choose. The kinds of experience I'd had at Wisconsin weren't even similar, although I'd been encouraged to continue from undergraduate to graduate studies of the dance while there. Approved approaches to my subject there seemed to be severely limited. That is, how could what I knew of human movement and the dance be translated into robotics? Or, what connection was there between the movements of Harlow's monkeys and that of human beings? The head of the dance department in Madison was partial to statistical analysis and 'scientific' experiments related to dancing carried out by means of a centrifuge housed on the top floor of Lathrop Hall. For example, when I inquired into the preferred subjects of Master's theses in the dance department, I discovered that one-hundred page analyses of steps, hops and jumps were highly considered — any subject that dealt with "data" and not the people who produced it. I was told that art (especially dancing) was *subjective*, science was *objective* and never the twain shall meet. I went to West Africa.

From there, I arrived in Matthew Arnold's "Beautiful city! ...whispering from her towers the last enchantments of the Middle Age. ... Home of lost causes, and forsaken beliefs, and unpopular names, and impossible loyalties!"[4] If my praise of Oxford seems too fulsome, it is because there — and only there — was I able to realize the dreams I'd had for as many years as I could remember, not the least of which was to elevate dancing to its rightful place among subjects worthy of a lifetime's study. An impossible dream? Maybe. A "lost cause?" Probably, but nonetheless important for all of that.

I thought I'd said all I had to say about dancing in the B.Litt. thesis and, two months before completing it, I began field work studies which were meant to be the centerpiece of my Doctoral study, entitled *Communities By Choice* about Carmelite

4 *Essays in Criticism*, First series (1865), *Preface*.

nuns and friars,[5] but this was not to be. Walking from the Institute towards St. John's College with Ardener on a crisp autumn day in November 1972, he asked, "How committed are you to doing Doctoral work on the Carmelites?"

"About as committed as one can be" I replied, wondering what would follow this opening conversational gambit.

"The faculty wonders if you'd continue your work on human movement at the Doctoral level" he said. "You've cleared all the underbrush in the B.Litt. and while I realize you may be a bit fed up with the subject of movement, you could develop it fully in a D.Phil. A monograph on the Carmelites, while interesting, would be a more traditional type of thesis — one that would reflect your capabilities as an anthropologist, true — but a thesis on movement would also demonstrate that, plus the fact that it is work that has never been done. You could carry out the work on religious orders at a post-Doctoral level, couldn't you?"

I couldn't refuse a request from people who had been unfailingly kind and considerate and to whom I owed so much. I could also see the common sense behind their suggestion: one couldn't very well carry out a practical program of attempts to develop a subfield of the anthropology of human movement studies from a standpoint of the anthropology of religion. So it was that work on the Doctoral degree began, culminating in March 1976 with the *viva voce* (the oral exams) which I enjoyed immensely. The *viva* still ranks as one of the best four-hour conversations I've ever had.

Writing the D.Phil. was pure unadulterated fun, partly because by this time, I knew how to write and I knew how to use the university to the best advantage. Writing a thesis may not be everyone's idea of fun, but it was mine, including all the intensity, the flow of energy, the development of ideas and the sheer joy of creation. The field research for the thesis, carried out in England, resulted in ethnographies of the Dominican Tridentine Mass, the ballet, Checkmate, and the Chinese Exercise Technique, T'ai Chi Ch'uan. Mr. Ardener was completely (although

---

5 One published essay resulted from the work I did: 'The Brides of Christ' in *Perceiving Women* (Ed. Shirley Ardener), London: Malaby, 1976, pp. 105-126.

always critically) supportive — a support I appreciated because he never attempted to create me or my subject in his own image and he took the trouble to find out what I wanted.

What did I want? The obvious answer was that I wanted to talk about dances and dancing in non-frivolous ways. I wanted to connect the act of dancing with other human movement-based modes of expression — sign languages, the martial arts, everyday movement, ritual, ceremonies and so forth. But my desire to talk and write about the dance was merely a surface structure beneath which the deep structures of my life lay, like the deeply excavated foundations of a castle or a skyscraper.

The vows I'd made at seventeen after realizing that I didn't know how to talk about what I knew and what I thought was important (see p. 19) were finally consummated at Oxford thirty-five years later. By the time I finished writing two theses, I not only knew how to talk about what I knew and thought was important, I could write about it as well. Apart from that, writing meant that the achievement was recorded: it was a social and political fact — a social fact because it was a recognized degree and a political fact: I was 'Doctor' Williams.

This is not to say I couldn't express myself 'pre-Oxford'. I could and did. My career as a professional dancer is testimony to that, but dancing is a different kind of expression: it is the *acting out* of a story, not the *telling* of it. In my opinion, and certainly in my life, both were vitally necessary.

After finishing the Doctoral thesis, I reluctantly left England the end of May 1976, to return to New York, thence to Boston, where Minor White lay dying. Three wealthy English friends (who requested anonymity) connected to the Institute of Cultural Research[6] bailed me out of an eight hundred pound overdraft I'd built up at Barclay's Bank early in 1975. If they hadn't paid the overdraft and supported me during the final year of writing, I would not have been able to finish the D.Phil.

---

6 Located in Tunbridge Wells, Kent, headed by the late Idries Shah, author of many books on Sufism.

I left Oxford before the formal graduation ceremonies in June because Minor wanted to see me. We did not know it then, but I arrived at his house five weeks before he died. Later, when I finally entered the door of my sister's house in Minnesota during the second week of July 1976, I was broke, in debt, and most of my clothing was threadbare. But, the quest I'd begun thirty years before was complete — almost to the day. It was on July twenty-seventh, 1946, that the detective told me of Mom's death. Although I'd managed to acquire intellectual and spiritual wealth beyond my wildest dreams in England, I was otherwise impoverished, but I didn't care.

To this day, I find it hard to tell anyone about what actually happened to me during the Oxford years. The most accurate description of the transformation I experienced as a result of my years-long quest is contained in a short essay (a "little *jeu d'esprit*" according to Garnett) by a mathematician, Edwin Abbott, whose *Flatland: A Romance of Many Dimensions*, was reprinted in 1962.

Assuming the character of a Square who lives in Flatland, he explains Pointland (which has no dimensions); Lineland (possessing one dimension) and Flatland (two dimensions) where he meets a Sphere, who takes him to Spaceland, the land of three dimensions, where he was

> introduced to the Cube, and I found that this marvellous Being was indeed no Plane, but a Solid; and that he was endowed with six plane sides and eight terminal points called solid angles ... Were I to give the Sphere's explanation of these matters, succinct and clear though it was, it would be tedious to an inhabitant of Space, who knows these things already. Suffice it, that by his lucid statements, and by changing the position of objects and lights, and by allowing me to feel the several objects ... he at last made all things clear to me, so that I could now readily distinguish between a Circle and a Sphere, a Plane figure and a Solid. This was the Climax, the Paradise, of my strange eventful History ... (Abbott 1962[1884]: 85).

Although Spaceland was the climax of the Square's strange eventful history, at the end of the story, the Square incurs the wrath of the Sphere by suggesting there are *four* dimensions (possibly many more); an idea the Sphere cannot tolerate because Spaceland is as rigidly bound by three dimensions as the Flatlanders' world is restricted by two. The Square ends up in prison.

> Prometheus up in Spaceland was bound for bringing down fire for mortals, but I — poor Flatland Prometheus — lie here in prison for bringing down nothing to my countrymen. Yet I exist in the hope that these memoirs, in some manner, I know not how, may find their way to the minds of humanity in Some Dimension, and may stir up a race of rebels who shall refuse to be confined to limited Dimensionality (1962[1884]: 101).

Although I'd discovered many additional dimensions-of-being through the experience with Chappell in Rochester, during the weekly visits to Dr. Wadro's office, and in Ghana through encountering a culture totally unlike my own, I longed for more. I always knew that other dimensions existed (how I knew, I am unable to explain), but Abbott's story is an apt metaphor. It resonates with me to this day because I am one of the "race of rebels who ... refuse to be confined to limited Dimensionality."

I was jerked out of my teen-age Flatland into the real world when I was sixteen. Everything I thought I knew and understood about people at that age was suddenly blown to kingdom-come. I found myself in a world where people *did* one thing but *said* another. I hadn't really noticed the discrepancies before.

Adults only rarely admitted mistakes. They often didn't know how to say what they *did* know because they were afraid, or, they couldn't conceive of re-editing the scripts into which they'd been born or those they developed as individuals during their "formative" years. As I would now express this problem, there are many who, having accepted some version of limited dimensionality, insist that those limitations are the sum total of reality.

I discovered that I didn't really love — or even like — many of those whom I believed I loved and that I liked things that many of those around me believed to be 'unnatural' (I didn't want to have children), 'idealistic' (I wanted to be an artist), or they simply classified what I wanted as insignificant.

Finally, I learned that most human potential is unrealized. Herein, of course, lies the significance of the whole thing.

Chapter 17

> I wanted to live deep and suck out all the marrow of life ... to drive life into a corner, and reduce it to its lowest terms, and, if it proved to be mean, why then to get the whole and genuine meanness of it, and publish its meanness to the world; or if it were sublime, to know it by experience; and be able to give a true account of it in my next excursion.
>
> (Henry David Thoreau, *Walden*, 1854)

When you've been to the absolute emotional bottom as I was most of the time for the better part of the years 1947 to 1956, you see everything from a distance. If you *cannot* see this way, you might commit suicide as I almost did because you can't see any way out of intolerable situations. Why didn't I commit suicide when I was eighteen? I didn't kill myself because, I reasoned, "if I kill myself, I lose the chance of finding out who I am and what I can do and be." Up to now I've never told anyone except Dr. Wadro about that, but I remember making the decision early in 1947 as clearly as if it happened yesterday.

Nobody who knew me in 1947 would have been surprised if Shirley Bowden had committed suicide, just as no one would have been surprised to find out later on in life that she had become an alcoholic, a drug addict or a prostitute. Perhaps the surprising thing is that neither my sister nor I succumbed to alcoholism, drug addiction or prostitution. Neither of us turned out as many people expected us to and this is why the significance of the story I've told is rooted in the idea of 'potential'

People live in narrow realities because they take their own and everyone else's consciousness for granted, just as they take the world as they see it for granted. My story begins at an instant when I couldn't take anything for granted. Suddenly, I had no home, no parents, no security — nothing. Everything I thought was real became unreal. Everything I thought I could depend upon no longer existed. I was betrayed by people whom I thought were real friends.

In other words, life drove me into a corner. Years later, after I understood what had happened, I wanted to drive life into a corner. I wanted to get my own back, and I did — by fighting for it. In 1946, I didn't even know what to fight for, where the battlefield was or what my enemies looked like. I was lost.

It was seeing (sensing, intuiting, imagining, believing or what-you-will) that there was something *more* about life as a whole that encouraged my revolt against relatives, socio-economic background and upbringing. I fled from the places I lived as a teen-ager and child just as I later fled from two husbands and family members (excepting my sister) for most of my life. There are those who say I did this because (understandably) no one would want to live with the painful associations those people and places awakened.

"You escaped and it's a good thing you did" they conclude.

Characteristically, I disagreed. I've never seen leaving Oregon solely as an escape. It's true that I ran away, but at the time, I ran *towards* something as yet undefined. *I wasn't running away.* I didn't always know specifically where my running or the many leaps in the dark I made would take me, but I never doubted that there was more to life than I was able to see on the surface at any given moment. And this, I think is the key: this 'more'. But, how can I define 'more'?

I always wanted more knowledge and more consciousness — more 'knowing together' which is literally what the word 'conscious' means.[1] I was seriously — for all I knew, terminally — hurt because of the narrow realities in which my parents lived which provided both the source and shapes of their conflicts. I didn't want to live either in theirs or my family's kinds of reality.

---

1 'Consciousness' is usually defined as 'awareness'; but this is an inferior definition which usually means little more than being physically awake in contrast to being asleep.

I had to find new ideas, *transforming* ideas, that would enable me to create new relations between myself and everything. Someone more imaginative and resourceful than I might have been able to find such ideas while remaining in familiar places with familiar people. I could not.

Later on I discovered that it isn't the external forms of one's life that count. It's how the forms are 'fleshed out' — how they are used to increase consciousness — that provides the important measure. There are people who have reached the kind of spiritual fulfillment I sought without moving around as I have done. I wouldn't want anyone to imitate anything I did in the vain hope that traveling or 'being a dancer', for example, is the one sure way toward inner growth and illumination. I discovered the 'more' there is to life through dancing, teaching dancing and, later on, through becoming a social anthropologist. There is nothing inherent in dancing, in social anthropology or in extensive traveling that predetermines that kind of outcome.

We create hopeless predicaments with reference to questions about the 'more' as I have defined it. No external vocation, profession or line of work provides a sure path. A Carmelite nun told me that she entered her monastery because she knew enough about herself to know that she needed strong external structures upon which to depend, not because she was assured of reaching her spiritual goals by becoming a contemplative nun. The sun shines equally upon all of us.

On the other hand, we live in times when value judgments are *verboten*, thus there are those who think there are no significant distinctions to be made between the kinds of lives we lead. The prevailing idea seems to be "anything goes as long as I accept people (myself included) as they are and let it go at that. Only weirdos, kooks and children try to live up to ideals. Forget about that. Look after Number One." Then, too, conceptual definition is unfashionable.

I recently heard an undergraduate say, "If I want to know something, all I have to do is find it on the Internet." I didn't say anything, but wondered if the world-wide web would have significantly helped the teen-aged Shirley Bowden in 1946, even if it had existed. I doubt it. Furthermore, these days, we've made our spoken communications even more difficult than they already are through the additional problem of being "politically correct" (whateverthatis). Even so, only a minority, I hope, are willing to accept the ethical relativism of cynics or the didactic prescriptions of 'true believers' as final answers.

One of the last words on the subject of what 'more' there is to this life surely goes to a survivor of concentration camps[2] who said that *existence falters unless it is lived in terms of transcendence towards something beyond itself.* Viktor Frankl maintained that human beings are responsible for the fulfilment of specific meanings in their personal lives, but, he added, people must be responsible *before* something, or *to* something, whether that 'something' is society, humanity or one's own conscience.

I began my life's story describing a moment that ended my life as I had known it. In that ending was a beginning. Taken together, beginning and ending enigmatically suggest that they contain one another — that they exist simultaneously. So many aspects of life do just that: birth/death, good/evil, pleasure/pain, buying/selling. About joy and sorrow, Kahlil Gibran asked,

> Is not the cup that holds your wine the
> very cup that was burned in the potter's oven?
>
> And is not the lute that soothes your
> spirit, the very wood that was hollowed with
> knives?[3]

The knives and the fire are integral parts of the cup, the wine and the lute. None exists without the other.

> It's curious how one can experience pain and
> joy simultaneously. Although my eyes were
> blindfolded, I sensed their fear — and rejoiced
> (pp. 8-9). ... In the long months of confinement,
> I often thought of how to transmit the pain that

---

2 Viktor Frankl. 1962. *Man's Search For Meaning.* Boston: Beacon Press.

3 Kahlil Gibran. 1963[1923]. *The Prophet.* New York: Knopf, p. 29.

> a tortured person undergoes. And always I concluded that it was impossible. ... A man is shunted so quickly from one world to another that he's unable to tap a reserve of energy so as to confront this unbridled violence. That is the first phase of torture: to take a man by surprise, without allowing him any reflex defense, even psychological. A man's hands are shackled behind him, his eyes blindfolded. No one says a word. Blows are showered upon a man. He's placed on the ground and someone counts to ten, but he's not killed. A man is then led to what may be a canvas bed, or a table, stripped, doused with water, tied to the ends of the bed or table, hands and legs outstretched. And the application of electric shocks begins. The amount of electricity transmitted by the electrodes — or whatever they're called — is regulated so that it merely hurts, or burns, or destroys. It's impossible to shout — you howl. ... (Jacobo Timerman, p. 33)[4]

I don't think I could have survived what Timerman endured. I managed to hold up under the teen-age trauma I went through and overcame it. My sister survived to overcome her totally different experience of the same event. Such stories are worth telling, I think, not because of the uniqueness or magnitude of the wounds inflicted or the pain endured. Thousands of men and women, including Frankl and Timerman have suffered and survived far worse pain than I did. For three years, Richard Wurmbrand was in solitary confinement in a cell thirty feet below ground near Bucharest, Rumania.[5]

Standing by a bombed-out city block in London (of which there were still many in the early 'fifties when I first went there), I've thought about the hundreds of people who left their homes one morning or evening, only to return sometime later to find everything gone — their homes reduced to smouldering

---

4 Jacobo Timerman. 1981. *Prisoner Without a Name, Cell Without a Number.* [Trans. T. Talbot]. New York: Knopf.

5 Richard Wurmbrand. 1971. *Sermons in Solitary Confinement.* London: Hodder & Stoughton.

heaps of rubble. I'm not the only one in the world who casually said "Goodbye, see you later!" never to see that person again.

There are worlds of difference, however, between the sixteen-year-old who said "See you later" to her mother the end of July 1946, and the forty-one-year-old who said goodbye to her friends in August 1970, before undertaking the ocean voyage that carried her from West Africa to England. Life drove the sixteen-year-old into a corner. The forty-one-year-old had already experienced a dozen years of "living deep and sucking out the marrow of life," and was quite capable of driving life into a corner, looking forward to 'more of the more' so to speak. The transformation occurred because she ceased being a victim of her own limited dimensionality, and, she accepted responsibility for her own life and actions.

Having said that, an aphorism comes to mind: "Writing a book is like scrubbing an elephant: there's no good place to begin or end, and it's hard to keep track of what you've already covered (*Anonymous*)." I want to end this book with a couple of ideas about beginnings. Ending the book by drawing attention to beginning (birth) makes sense because I began with an ending (death).

To most people (perhaps especially to women), 'birth' means the birth of a child. I never had children and never regretted the fact that I didn't. In the late 'forties and early 'fifties, women couldn't choose to have or not have children as easily as they can now. I recall being treated to unsolicited lectures in which dire prophecies were made: "Your life will be meaningless. You'll never feel really fulfilled." In general, my well-meaning, self-appointed behavior-monitors made life miserable. What if they were right? Could a female of the species be a real woman if she didn't have children?

For a short time while I was married to Olly, the temptation to have a child simply to find out what the experience was like was strong, but I didn't give in. Thank God I didn't, because that's the wrong reason (among a multitude of wrong reasons) for having children. When I returned to the United States in 1976, I could talk about my childless state with impunity: "I didn't have babies, I had a Doctoral thesis instead." As early as 1959, I could say, "I didn't have babies, I had a dance company instead." Women are capable of giving life to many things besides children.

Most people wouldn't dream of limiting men's creative faculties and capacities to the fathering of children, nor would they say that 'manhood' depends solely upon the condition of being a father. In contrast, for many centuries, the essence of womanhood has been placed solely in her biology — in her child-bearing capacity, not only in our own but in other cultures. Let me hasten to say that I'm not subtracting any of the praise or the glory owed to women who bear and look after children. I don't minimize the vocation of motherhood in any way: there is a sense in which I, like everyone else, owe my existence to it; however, I don't believe that 'womanhood' and 'motherhood' are synonymous, nor do I believe the concepts are interchangeable. The former may include the latter, but not the other way around.

On a lesser level, I merely report that I'm not now, and never have been, the kind of person best-suited to having children. This doesn't mean I'm not capable of work, self-sacrifice, hope and effort. These are all requirements for parenthood, to be sure, but they are requirements for other things too. I work hard and put forth prodigious efforts to assist students towards greater understanding, whether I'm teaching dancing, social anthropology or both. I sacrificed material comforts to create and maintain a dance company. I literally impoverished myself during the process of writing the Doctoral thesis, the guts of which is 'semasiology': a theory of human action that has since proved useful to those seeking new ways of understanding human movement: dances, ceremonies, rituals, sign languages or the martial arts. That theory is my brain-child. Of the many things I've accomplished, it is, in my estimation, my crowning achievement.

All births require physical labor — vast expenditures of energy and sacrifice. They require seeing familiar things in new ways and struggling to overcome limitations and disabilities on all levels. I'm unable to assess which is more soul-, or heartrending: the nine months of misery and the pain of prolonged labor that some women tell me they experienced when their first child was born, or the months (often years) of anguish, followed by the pain of producing a new self-identity, a new theory — anything that is creatively substantial and benefits others. Is it really necessary to elevate one kind of birth over all others?

Finally, having reduced life to its lowest terms, has it proved to be 'mean' or 'sublime'? Not unexpectedly, I'd have to say I've found life to be *both* mean *and* sublime. A true account of life as I have lived it doesn't conform to the law of the excluded middle. It isn't 'digital', it's analogic: it isn't 'either-or', it's both — and ever so much more — provided we don't lose our Selves in the finite games of limited dimensionality.

Epilogue

> Not that the story need not be long,
> but it will take a long time to make it short.
> (Thoreau, 'Letter to Mr. B.', 16 November, 1867)

It would be unfair to leave readers with the July 1976, image of me standing at my sister's door in Minnesota "broke, in debt, [and with] most of my clothing ... threadbare" (p. 186). Twenty-two years have passed since then. My debts are small, I'm not penniless, and my clothing isn't threadbare. During the intervening years, I travelled around the world twice and taught anthropology of human movement studies in universities in the United States, Australia and East Africa. I lived, learned and experienced more, I think, than I was able to teach.

The tale of those years — travelling, doing research, meeting many people whom I grew to know and love — the whole shimmering cascade of events, including a bout with breast cancer in Australia, "need not be long" but they would require another book to do them justice.

All my attempts to summarize everything in an epilogue have come to nothing. It took a long time to make the story of my first forty-eight years short enough to contain in a single book. One day soon, I hope to begin writing another.

In the meantime, I think about something Ernest Hemingway said that Marlene Dietrich quoted in A.E. Hotchner's Papa Hemingway (pt. 1, chap. 1 - 1966 edition): "Never confuse movement with action." "In those five words," she added, "he gave me a whole philosophy."

I've spent most of a lifetime thus far trying to work out the differences between movement and action, and I reached a conclusion: regardless of what the post-modernists say, 'experience' isn't a matter of being a dancer, or traveling around the world, or being a convict's daughter — or whatever. Experience isn't what happens to you.

Experience is what you do with what happens.

That's what counts.

Index

AUTHORS

Abbott, Edwin, 186
Arnold, Matthew, 155

Baum, Frank L., 25
Blake, William, 5-6
Browning, Robert, 43

Chesterton, G.K., 94

Eliot, T.S., 33, 45, 53, 63
Evans-Pritchard, E. E., 182

Frankl, Viktor, 192

Gibran, Kahlil, 192

Hoffman, Michael, 111-12
Hotchner, A. E., 197

Ibsen, Henrick, 131

Lienhardt, Godfrey, 170

Millay, Edna St. Vincent, 23

Sanai, Hakim, 115

Santayana, George, 179
Shakespeare, William, (Macbeth), 1; (Othello), 11, (Merchant of Venice), 79; (Richard II), 20
Shaw, George Bernard, 170

Thoreau, Henry David, 189, 197
Timerman, Jacobo, 193

White, Minor, 105, 111
Williams, Drid, 130, 177, 184
Woolfe, Virginia, 143
Wurmbrand, Richard, 193

SUBJECTS

American Legion, 24, 26
  Drum Corps, 35

Art Museum (Portland), 61
  and job as a model, 21, 62
  and modeling in New York, 87

Baffling Detective Story, 15-18

Baker City (Oregon), 47
  and bicycle, 49-50
  Carnegie Library, 48-9
  St. Francis Academy, 48

Chappell, Walter, 103, 105-6
  and equivalence, 105, 110
  and many photographs, 107-8
  and seeing mass of selves, 108
  and 'thick' time, 109-110

Choice
  element in dance therapy, 124, 126
  essential point of therapy, 127
  'key word', 101
  ~ at Oxford, 183

Christmas Eve, 31
  in 1946, 51

Cornucopia, 28, 36, 44
  winter in, 44-5
  school in, 48

Cousins (Darlene, Beryl, Helen and Jackie Koopman), 29-30
  Helen and 4H, 33-4

Dance, 21
  'carrying coals to Newcastle', 146
  and 'dumb' dancers, 127
  and classroom directions, 121
  and economic plight of dancers, 86
  and philosophy, 127
  and ruptured tendon, 114-15
  creating a ~ (Forms One), 116-17
  Experience Anonyme (Wisconsin), 123
  teaching a ~ class in Ghana, 137-38
  teaching professionals, 120
  ~ company in Ghana, 147-149
  ~ teaching techniques, 121
  ~ therapy, 122-3

Dances
  and social anthropology, 169; (contrast to U.W.), 183
  ballroom ~, 150
  Dance of the Bedu Moon, 144, 152, 158; (Bedu masks), 159
  Ewe *Agbekɔ*, 147-48
  Gbain dance, 158; (and mask), 158
  Sokodae: Come and Dance, 151-52

Dancing,
  'rooms' for ~, 118
  ballet ~ (Portland), 61
  reasons for ~, 128
  teaching ~ for Joffrey in N.Y., 87
  ~ and Dr. Taylor (Portland), 61
  ~ at University of Wisconsin, 122

Emotion
  and double consciousness, 2, 20
  emotion~ levels, 99-100
  ~al 'flash-freeze', 2
  ~s in dance therapy, 125

England
and absence when father died, 81
and first trip to, 69, 87
and state-supported arts, 85-6
and departure from, 185

England (people)
Audrey de Vos, 84
Beryl Grey, 84
Dame Kathleen Kenyon, 166
Dame Ninette de Valois, 84-5
Marie Rambert, 84-5
E. E. Evans-Pritchard, 152, 154, 156, 160, 165, 171; (as E. P.), 177-78; (attitudes toward anthropology), 182-83

England (places)
H.M.S. *Aureole* (ship), 164-65
Institute of Cultural Research (Kent) 185
Institute of Social Anthropology, 166; (common room), 170 71
Liverpool Museum, 160, 165
Oxford (City of), 154-55, 161; (arrival in), 166
Royal Anthropological Society Library (London), 152, 154
Sadler's Wells School, 69, 84
St. Hugh's College, 161; (graduate house), 178
St. Macrina and St Gregory Houses, 180

Experience
(dimensions of being),187;
(more of life), 190;
(transcendence), 192;
(what counts in),197

Farm
("the ranch") in Halfway, 4, 28, 29, 30

Father (Wes Bowden)
as AFL steward, 45
as 'buckaroo', 54
as host, 27
~s admissions of guilt, 8-9
~s anger, 80
~s death, 77
~s freak accident, 43-4
~s funeral, 81
~s hands, 42, 44
~s hopes for parole, 65
~s lawyer (Patterson), 52
~s marriage, 55-6
~s mother, 'Nana', 54-5
~s pardon by Governor, 77, 79
~s support of Nana, 54
~s trust in older daughter, 53, 62

Flatland, 186-87
(limited dimensions), 187;
(narrow realities), 190

Ghana, 129
a ~ian dance class, 137-38
Adzido (dance company), 147, 149

amoebic dysentery, 141
arrival in ~, 132
Ashanti gold weights, 162
bargaining in ~, 164
cooking yams, 132
fou-fou, 131, 134, 136
Hausa traders in ~, 161-63
Lobi greeting ceremony in ~, 134
obruni(s), 145-46
traditional ~ian concepts, 145
translation problems in ~, 130, 136
~ian drums, 143
~ian yams, 131-2, 135

Ghana (people in)
David Akele (cook-steward), 139-40, 141, 144
Dr. Carleen O'Loughlin (Paddy), 153-54, 155, 164-65
Father Han Steemers, 151-52, 156
Mr. Opoku, 128-9; (arguments with), 148-49, 156
Mustapha Tettey Addy, 142-43; (and Islam), 144, 157; 156, 164
Roy Seiber, 157, 161, 163

Ghana (places in)
Anyako, ~, 129
Institute of African Studies, 133
Ketekrachi, ~, 132, 141, 151
Lawra, ~, 134
University of ~, 128

Volta River, 132
Winneba, ~, 149-51

Grandfather
maternal, 50-1
paternal, 54-5

Grandmother ("Grammy")
~s and Grandpa's farm, 49
~s attitude toward father, 20
~s garden, 50
~s grief, 18

Hearst Newspapers, 6
American Weekly, 64, 67-8
trial with ~, 66-7

Ivory Coast, 130, 144; (Sorobongo), 157; (Tambi), 157; (border with Ghana), 159; 160

Jefferson High School, 47
and honor roll, 57
and 'smoker', 58
and sororities, 56-7
and teenage conformity, 59
and 'uniform', 57

Judges
Tooze, 69
Hawkins, 69

Lawyers
Hall, John H., 69, 76

Jordon, Robert, 66, 68
Patterson, J.R., 52; (emphasis on death sentence), 65-6
trust of father's ~, 52

Letters (reproduced)
Gov. Paul Patterson to Wes Bowden, 76
H.M. Randall to Judge Tooze, 72
J. M. Randall to John Hall, 75
John Hall to Parole Board, 73-75
John Hall to Warden Alexander, 70
Judge Tooze to Drid, 72
Judge Tooze to Parole Board, 71-2

Little House on the Prairie, 47

Mormon Basin, 37-8, 47, 51
catalogues, 38
hoist at mine, 41
mine shaft, 40
rattlesnake, 39-40

Mother (Fern Bowden)
and books, 60
as symbol to me, 52
as teetotaler, 56
~s beatings, 54
~s excellence as hostess, 27
~s faults, 54
~s funeral, 18-19
~s marriage 56

Music, 31, 35-6

Name, 'Shirley' or 'Drid', 24

New York
and move to, 101
and Rochester, N.Y., 103, 106, 111
and studio in, 87
grew up in ~, 116
memories of ~, 88
return trip to ~ from Portland, 96
~s Chinatown, 103
~s Coney Island, 102
~s docks, 102
~s New Dance Theater, 88
~s Staten Island Ferry, 102

Oosterbeek, Holland, 153

Oxford University, 166
'Mr. Tyler's science', 177
Diploma (students) 167, 169, 175;
(exams), 179-80
Doctoral degree, 184-85
Edwin Ardener, 169, 175-76;
(supervisor), 180;
(and B.Litt.), 181;
(and D.Phil.), 185
exams, (preparation), 178;
(dream), 179;
(papers for ~), 180
Godfrey Lienhardt, 172;
(tutorial), 174, 177-78

Institute of Social Anthropology, 166;
(common room), 170-71
John Beattie (tutorial), 175-76
Malcolm Crick (advice), 173; 175-76
New College, 176
questions for weekly papers, 172-73
Rom Harré (philo. of science), 176
St. Hugh's College, 161
teaching methods, 175

Pandora Box Murder, 6, 9, 64

'Pidgin' English, 140-41

Police questioning, 14-15

Ross, Dorian, 63-65, 83, 86, 94
and betrayal, 97
and divorce, 94, 98-9, 101
and Nona, 92, 94-5, 98
and nurses, 91-2
and Portland hospital, 90

Sister (Doris)
and Dad's departure and words of caution, 12-13, 21
and embalming, 81
and Governor Paul Patterson, 77
and suffering, 14, 81
~s early marriage, 7

~s interviews with jury members, 69, 76
~s ordeal, 2, 3, 4
~s statement about father's jury, 82
~s statement about father, 81

Social Anthropology
~ changed thinking, 182

Sumpter, Oregon, 36, 47, 51

Teachers' Training College (Ghana), 149-50.

Tuffy (Black Angus calf), 34-5

Vows
about speaking, 19, 181, 185
jealousy, 10

Wadro, Dr. H.S., 20, 21, 52, 89-90, 95
~ and end of therapy, 112-13
~ and joining Women's Air Force, 97
~ and successful therapy, 100
~ and suicide, 189
~ and the Land of Oz, 113-14
~s protected atmosphere, 99-100

Washington St. house (Baker), 25
and bridge parties, 25

and dinner table, 27-8
and paper dolls, 24-5
baby Doris, 24
dinners, 47

Williams, Oliver P. (Olly), 8, 86, 98

White, Minor
~s 'continuous soup-pot', 107
~s *Sequence 17* (photographs), 111
last visit to ~, 186

Wisconsin School for Girls, 126
~ and dance therapy, 122-3

Women
and birth, 194-95
and 'womanhood', 195

World War II, 46
Pearl Harbor, 47
Arnhem, Holland, 153

Writing, 181
CarmeliteOrder, 184;
(scrubbing an elephant), 194

Yamhill St. house (Portland), 1, 3, 8, 11 (basement of), 12-14; 17

About The Author

Drid Williams was born October 12, 1928 in St. Elizabeth's Hospital, Baker, Oregon. Forty-eight years later, she completed three graduate degrees in social anthropology (Diploma, B. Litt. and D.Phil.) from St. Hugh's College, Oxford, U.K. between 1970 and 1976.

Before becoming an anthropologist, she was a professional dancer, beginning her career in 1948 as a teacher and choreographer in Portland, Oregon, where she and her second husband were an exhibition ballroom dance-team. She continued her dance career in New York City where she maintained a studio from 1956-1962., originating a small touring company, *The Circle Dancers.*

Her career as a professional dancer was terminated by a ruptured left achilles tendon in 1962. Recuperating with her sister, who lives in Minnesota, she moved to Madison, Wisconsin, where she taught for the University's Extension Division throughout the state from 1963-66, when she had the opportunity to teach at the Institute of African Studies (University of Ghana, Legon, Accra). After residing in West Africa from February 1967 to August 1970, she went to Oxford at the suggestion of E.E. Evans-Pritchard to study social anthropology.

Returning to the United States in 1976, Williams taught for two semesters at the University of Pennsylvania, then directed graduate programs in the anthropology of the dance and human movement studies at New York University (1979-1984) and Indiana University (1984-85), where she also completed a Master's degree in Library Science. She then taught at the University of Sydney (Australia - 1986-1990) and Moi University and U.S. International University (Kenya - 1991-1993). She returned to Minnesota in November, 1993, to be with her sister, whose husband died in June 1994. She presently divides her time between writing and editing teaching texts in the anthropology of human movement, teaching Dance History at the University of Minnesota and working part-time as a process-server for *Metro Legal, Inc.* in Minneapolis.

She is the architect of a theory of human actions (Semasiology) and is both founder and senior editor for the *Journal for the Anthropological Study of Human Movement* [JASHM], now in its tenth volume has existed since 1980. She is the author of many published articles in her field and has so far produced three books: *Ten Lectures on Theories of the Dance* (Scarecrow Press, 1991), *Visual Anthropology: The Signs of Human Action* 8(2-4), 1996 and *Anthropology and Human Movement, 1: The Study of Dances* (Scarecrow Press, 1997). The fourth, *Anthropology and Human Movement, 2: Searching For Origins*, is in preparation.

About the Publisher

High Ground Publishing, a division of Northwoods Consulting, has as its mission the publication of previously unpublished works **that recognize, uplift and celebrate the heroic nature of human life from a rational, reasoned and objective point of view, free of mysticism and magic.**

Manuscripts that meet these requirements will receive a serious evaluation. Adult nonfiction preferred, fiction considered. No poetry or books for children.

Manuscripts must include SASE if the author wants it returned.

No agents, authors only.

Order Form

To order additional copies of *Beyond Survival*, send a check or money order ($17.95 plus $3.00 shipping and handling, $20.95 total) made payable to:

NORTHWOODS CONSULTING
6107 S. W. Murray Blvd., Suite 351
Beaverton, Oregon 97008-4467

Please send a copy of *Beyond Survival* to:

Date _____

Name _____

Street Address _____

_____

City _____ State _____ ZIP _____

VISA/MasterCard Number

_____

Expiration Date _____

Signature _____